Strengthening the Heartbeat

Thomas J. Sergiovanni

Strengthening the Heartbeat

Leading and Learning Together in Schools

JOSSEY-BASS
A Wiley Imprint
www.josseybass.com

Published by Jossey-Bass
A Wiley Imprint
989 Market Street, San Francisco, CA 94103-1741   www.josseybass.com

Jossey-Bass books and products are available through most bookstores. To contact Jossey-Bass directly, call our Customer Care Department within the U.S. at 800-956-7739, outside the U.S. at 317-572-3986, or fax 317-572-4002.

Jossey-Bass also publishes its books in a variety of electronic formats. Some content that appears in print may not be available in electronic books.

Library of Congress Cataloging-in-Publication Data

Sergiovanni, Thomas J.
  Strengthening the heartbeat: leading and learning together in schools / Thomas J. Sergiovanni.— 1st ed.
    p. cm. — (The Jossey-Bass education series)
  Includes bibliographical references and index.
  ISBN 0-7879-6544-8 (alk. paper)
  1. School management and organization—United States. 2. Educational leadership—United States. I. Title. II. Series.
  LB2805.S533 2004
  371.2'00973—dc22

                        2004008930

Printed in the United States of America
FIRST EDITION
HB Printing 10 9 8 7 6 5 4 3 2 1

Contents

Preface: Strengthening the Heartbeat

. . . .

Recently Lesley Iura at Jossey-Bass asked me if I would write a second edition of *Value-Added Leadership,* a book originally published in 1990. As work began it became clear that over the last fourteen years too much had happened in school leadership and improvement and too much had happened in how I think about those topics. It was time for an overhaul, not a revision. Though *Strengthening the Heartbeat: Leading and Learning Together* remains committed to value-added leadership, its understanding of how this idea works for school improvement has changed.

The Concept of Value-Added Leadership

To many readers, *value-added* sounds like a mouthful. What does it mean in plain English? Actually, the term has two meanings: one from economics and the other from moral reasoning.

Value-Added as an Economic Concept

Economists often ask, "What is the value of something?" and "How can we add more value to what we have?" In the corporate world, value-added is a seminal concept that provides a theory of management devoted to economic expansion. Owning a lot on the busy downtown corner of Smith and Vine, for example, enhances your financial portfolio. Putting a building on this lot to accommodate shops and restaurants adds value. Similarly, improving schools usually involves adding value to what we already have.

Though occasional reformers threaten to nuke the school or to adopt change strategies that jolt the system, in the end the prevailing strategy is to rely on a school's existing strengths and to build capacity by developing a collaborative culture of continuous improvement. When good teachers, for example, become better because of the in-class coaching that is provided, value is added. When teams of principals and teachers (and sometimes the superintendent too) engage in regularly scheduled learning walks in schools and process this experience with teachers, value is added to the traditional ways that we think about supervision and professional development. Value-added leaders ask: "What is the value to the school, its teachers, and its students when we continue to use a particular strategy?" and then, "How can we develop a better strategy that adds more value?" This question is followed by: "How can we build the capacity of people so that this better strategy gets implemented properly?" When this happens value-added leadership becomes a part of the everyday life of the school.

Value-Added as Moral Reasoning

In moral reasoning, value-added has different but equally powerful meanings. Value-added calls attention to that which is intrinsically important and desirable, as in "What values do we believe should guide our actions?" "What values define us, give us a sense of significance, and provide the norms that anchor our lives in a culture of meaning?" Moral reasoning is concerned with identifying and using the virtues, norms, and codes that bind people to a set of ideas in such a way that their relationships change. They become *bonded*, closer together, and feel morally obliged to help each other as they embody similar ideas and values. They become communities characterized by sacred ties of reciprocal obligations and responsibilities. In this moral context value-added leadership means the linking of management strategies to virtues, norms, codes, and other values that bring people together for leadership and learning.

The Lifeworld and the Systemsworld

Value-added leadership as moral reasoning is reflected in the *life-world* of schools. Value-added leadership as a strategy for achieving our purposes is reflected in the *systemsworld* of schools (see, for example, Sergiovanni, 2000). Both worlds are needed for schools to be effective. But, says the German philosopher and sociologist Jürgen Habermas (1987), it is the lifeworld that must drive the systemsworld. It is the stuff of culture, the essence of values and beliefs, the expression of needs, purposes, and desires of people and the sources of deep satisfaction in the form of meaning and significance that are experienced by parents, teachers, and students that define the lifeworld of schools. The systemsworld is important too. This is a world of instrumentalities, of inventing efficient ways and means that can help us achieve our ends. The systemsworld provides the foundation for the development of management, of organization, and of financial structures and strategies that provide the means for us to achieve our ends. Here's how the questions sort themselves out:

Lifeworld Concerns

What are our purposes?
Do they reflect what
  we believe?
How do they enhance
  meaning?
Are our lifeworld concerns
responsive to the needs of
students, teachers, and
other constituents?

Systemsworld Concerns

How do we achieve our purposes?
What strategies should
  we develop?
How effective are they?

What assessments do we need?

The lifeworld of the school is its heartbeat. This heartbeat is weakened whenever the systemsworld determines the lifeworld—whenever our means determine the ends rather than the other way around. In today's schools, for example, our purposes, the curriculum we teach, how we spend time, and even how we teach are increasingly being determined by the standardized assessments that distant authorities require us to administer.

Leadership and learning are ways in which we can strengthen the heartbeat so that the school is better able to grow itself on one hand and to serve its purposes on the other. "In sum, the lifeworld is the essence of hope. The systemsworld is the means to achieve hope. Both are necessary for schools to flourish. Schools can be the front lines in the defense of hope by maintaining proper balance. Achieving this balance . . . may be the most important purpose of leadership" (Sergiovanni, 2000, p. xix). And achieving this balance reinforces the heartbeat, increases its resilience, and helps it to bring leadership and learning together. If there were a formula for school success it would be to balance the lifeworld and strengthen the heartbeat of a school as a way to bring together leadership and learning.

Content of the Book

The Introduction reviews the value-added approach—recapping its basic principles and the nine dimensions and two corollaries that support its practice. Readers have a choice. They may revisit the concept and note the links provided between *Value-Added Leadership* and *Strengthening the Heartbeat* or they may go to Chapter One and pick up the heartbeat theme directly.

A strong heartbeat is a school's best defense against the obstacles leaders face as they seek to improve schools. Chapter One notes that this strengthening will require a new understanding of leadership, how it works, the nature of its relationship to learning, and why we need to practice both leadership and learning together. Key to this understanding will be the unveiling of the collective mindscapes that dominate our thinking about leadership, learning, and culture—the metaphors we use, our theories of practice, and other seminal issues that shape our reality. Leadership, Chapter One argues, requires the reconstruction of these mindscapes that define our work. Once these mindscapes from the head are shared, they begin to program the minds of people in such a way that a collective image of reality is created. If properly reconstructed, this reality can provide the instructional coherence, the organizational coherence, and the leadership coherence that schools need to succeed.

Chapter Two pushes us beyond shared leadership to leadership as an earned entitlement. Those with the necessary competence and commitment, for example, are entitled to lead. Leadership as entitlement is best understood within the context of reciprocal role relationships. Roles are not just markers that help define what a person should do, they are definers of covenants too. Roles as covenants work when we feel morally obliged to meet our responsibilities even when we do not want to or even whether we are getting something in exchange or not.

The theme of Chapter Three is making visions useful. For visions to work, they need to be turned into action statements. These action statements provide pathways for what needs to be done and become standards for evaluating effectiveness. When schools are able to do this they become transformed from ordinary organizations to communities of responsibility.

Adlai Stevenson High School in Lincolnshire, Illinois, is used as an example of how a school can turn visions into action statements that not only detail what each constituent group needs to do for the school's visions to be realized but obligates them to embody these action statements in their practice. The roles theme is revisited in Chapter Three. A covenant of obligations, it is argued, raises the stakes from management commitments to moral commitments. When a moral threshold is reached, teachers, parents, students, and administrators accept their roles and the elements that define them. Roles come from expectations that serve as a compass pointing the way and a beacon lighting the way. Expectations are not only received but also sent. Leadership under these conditions uses roles, role relationships, and role sets as the motivation for various constituent groups to work together to make visions a reality.

One way to strengthen the heartbeat of a school is by relying on virtues. Chapter Four examines four powerful leadership virtues: hopefulness, trust, piety, and civility. These virtues help transform school cultures and enable schools to achieve academic success within a caring environment. Using the Gompers Elementary School in Detroit as an example, the virtue of hopefulness is examined. Gompers succeeds because it has become a community of hope. But for hope to be a tool for school improvement it needs to be understood as something different from wishful thinking. Chapter Four concludes by examining the importance of relational trust in providing the social capital and other supports that are needed for schools to succeed. The importance of trust is widely accepted—but surprisingly trust is not as evident in practice as it should be.

Strategies for change typically begin with vision first and get around to building trust later. But effective strategies begin with trust first, then move to strategy and action. When it becomes time for implementation, the proper relationships have already been established. Yet in most schools when it becomes time to implement a school improvement initiative, everything stops while trust issues are dealt with. In the first case trust is used to forge new initiatives for improving effectiveness. In the second case efforts are on trying to mend fences as a way to improve relationships and trying to get people on board to improve their effectiveness. The power of several other virtues in bringing about change is also examined in Chapter Four.

If someone you knew said that they believed in a teacher-centered approach to schooling, it's likely that you would respond, "Wait a minute. I thought schools should be student centered. Isn't schooling all about the kids?" Chapter Five concedes that it is indeed all about the kids—but points out that a student-centered school only works when this centeredness is built within a larger framework of teacher-centeredness. The research on what counts in bringing about school improvement has produced evidence suggesting that little happens without a teaching staff that is highly motivated, competent, and committed. Chapter Five provides an argument for teacher-centeredness by suggesting that rarely does leadership directly affect school results variables. Instead, the more common pattern is indirect leadership that changes certain mediating variables in positive ways. Teachers account for a large chunk of these mediating variables. It is how these variables are affected that determines what the learning results for students will be. When it comes to improving student achievement, leadership has a stealth quality to it.

The title of Chapter Six is "Collaborative Cultures and Organizational Competence." Given this title it is no surprise that the Adlai Stevenson High School in Lincolnshire, Illinois, is used as an example of how to build an effective collaborative culture. The strength of Stevenson's culture relies on the deliberate efforts of designated leaders to build collaborative cultures as well as the conditions that are needed for them to function. But Stevenson and other places with successful cultures do not rely on leadership pushed from the top. Leadership bubbles up from the bottom too. That is, teachers willingly, voluntarily, and consistently help each other to be more effective, share their practice, and function as communities of practice.

Communities of practice bubble up from the bottom and collaborative cultures trickle down from the top. Designated leaders deliberately shape the nature of collaborative cultures. Teachers come together as communities of practice because they want to and because they believe that this level of collegiality is best for them and for the students they serve. Stevenson's ability to bring the trickling down of collaborative cultures and the bubbling up of communities of practice together serves as an archetype for leading and learning together.

Idea-based leadership, argues Chapter Seven, provides a more powerful foundation for leadership in a school than does mandated leadership, leadership based on position, or leadership based on personality. While all four have legitimate roles to play, it is ideas that belong at the center. When ideas back up leadership, a source of authority with moral overtones is created. This chapter shows how idea-based leadership works and describes eight basic competencies that leaders must have in order to successfully use idea-based leadership.

Like it or not, the fact is that leadership training and other efforts to improve leadership behavior can take us only so far. Leaders also bring to their work certain personality characteristics that may be more immutable than most of us think. Chapter Eight examines this issue and discusses three leadership archetypes: artists (great visionaries), craftsmen (great at getting things done), and technocrats (great at scripting whatever they touch). These archetypes were identified by Canadian researcher Patricia Pitcher. She found that it was the craftsman leader who had the most to do with effectiveness in organizations. Included in Chapter Eight is an inventory that will help you to reflect on your own approaches to leadership and on the approaches of your colleagues. Chapter Eight also includes a discussion of four stages of leadership (bartering, building, binding, and bonding) with each matched to different situations.

Acknowledgments

The basic idea behind this book is that schools should invest in developing a culture where leading and learning together is a core school improvement strategy. As is the case with many good ideas, today's interest in bringing the two together has its origins in practice. Dozens of outstanding school leaders might be mentioned as pioneers. The work of Anthony Alvarado, Elaine Fink, and others at District 2 in New York, Lucy Calkins from Teachers College, Columbia, Lauren Resnick from the University of Pittsburgh, Deborah Meier and her colleagues from District 4 in New York City and now Mission Hill in Boston, Melody Johnson from Providence, Rhode Island, Richard DuFour, Dan Galloway, and others at the Adlai Stevenson High School in Lincolnshire, Illinois, as well as the work of scholars such as Richard Elmore are particularly important. This book is based on a simple premise. Strengthening the heartbeat of a school is important. This strengthening is best done by investing in leading and learning together. This investment, in turn, will lead to higher levels of student achievement.

Special thanks to my assistant, Ruby Dehls, who with deft hands managed this project from beginning to end.

San Antonio, Texas   Thomas J. Sergiovanni
June 2004

The Author

Thomas J. Sergiovanni is Lillian Radford Professor of Education and Administration at Trinity University, San Antonio, Texas. He received his B.S. degree (1958) in elementary education from the State University of New York, Geneseo; his M.A. degree (1959) in educational administration from Teachers College, Columbia University; and his Ed.D. degree (1966), also in educational administration, from the University of Rochester.

From 1958 to 1964, he was an elementary school teacher and science consultant in New York State and taught in the teacher education program at the State University of New York, Buffalo. In 1966, he began nineteen years on the faculty of educational administration at the University of Illinois, Urbana-Champaign, where he chaired the department for seven years.

At Trinity University, Sergiovanni teaches in the school leadership program and in the five-year teacher education program. He is senior fellow at the Center for Education Leadership and the founding director of the Trinity Principals' Center. A former associate editor of *Educational Administration Quarterly*, he serves on the editorial board of the *Journal of Personnel Evaluation in Education* and *Catholic Education: A Journal of Inquiry and Practice*. Among his publications are *Moral Leadership: Getting to the Heart of School Improvement* (1992), *Building Community in Schools* (1994), *Leadership for*

the School House: How Is It Different? Why Is It Important? (1996),
The Lifeworld of Leadership: Creating Culture, Community, and Personal Meaning in Our Schools (2000), *The Principalship: A Reflective Practice Perspective*, 4th ed. (2001), *Leadership: What's in It for Schools?* (2001), and *Supervision: A Redefinition* (2002).

Strengthening the Heartbeat

Introduction

· ·

Value-Added Leadership Redux

The Nine Dimensions and Two Corollaries That Help Us Lead and Learn Together

Value-added leadership is key to strengthening a school's heartbeat. The principles of value-added leadership are as simple as they are powerful. They represent a set of ideas that have withstood the test of time despite the coming and going of leadership fads. Sometimes the principles sound a bit like "motherhood and apple pie," causing many to conclude that they are too virtuous to be taken seriously. For some they are difficult to talk and write about; therefore, their appearance in general management literature and in curricula of schools of education has been slow. Recent studies of successful schools and corporations, however, have begun to change this picture. These studies show that successful leaders not only understand value-added principles, they practice them with a vengeance.[1] They know that strengthening the heartbeat of

---

[1] In the 1980s, perhaps the five best-known books describing leadership and life in successful corporations and schools were *Corporate Cultures* (Deal and Kennedy, 1982), *In Search of Excellence* (Peters and Waterman, 1982), *Leaders: The Strategies for Taking Charge* (Bennis and Nanus, 1985), *The Good High School* (Lightfoot, 1983), and *Successful Schools for Young Adolescents* (Lipsitz, 1984).

This introduction provides an overview of the key principles and corollaries in *Value-Added Leadership: How to Get Extraordinary Performance in Schools* (Sergiovanni, 1990). It appeared as Chapter Two in the original and has been slightly edited and updated for this volume.

their organization is key to building a culture of leadership and learning.

This Introduction provides a basic framework for value-added leadership, comprising nine value-added dimensions with corresponding value dimensions and two corollaries. Though successful school leaders know the importance of value-added, often the audiences they serve (school boards, state bureaucrats, politicians, and so on) do not, demanding instead exclusive attention to value dimensions. Successful school leaders handle this problem by saying and doing some things to get the legitimacy and freedom they need, which then enables them to say and do other things that count toward quality schooling. The two corollaries are provided to help understand this seemingly contradictory slice of organizational reality. The basic framework for value-added leadership as proposed in the original book is outlined in the following list:

Value Dimensions The emphasis is on:	Value-Added Dimensions The emphasis is on:
1. Management	Leadership
2. Participation investment	Extraordinary performance investment
3. Manipulating situations	Providing symbols and enhancing meaning
4. Planning	Purposing
5. Giving directions	Enabling teachers and the school
6. Providing a monitoring system	Building an accountability system
7. Extrinsic motivation	Intrinsic motivation

8. Congeniality   Collegiality

9. Calculated leadership   Leadership by outrage

The Two Corollaries

1. Build in Canvas

2. Emphasize Moral Leadership

Key to the concept of value-added leadership is understanding that one should not have to choose between value and value-added. Both dimensions of leadership are needed if schools are to measure up to minimum standards and also to reach out to achieve a level of performance and success that is beyond expectations—indeed extraordinary. The value dimensions determine the competence side of the ledger. Their presence ensures that schools will function in a competent manner. The inevitable consequence of their absence is incompetence. But competence and excellence are not the same. School excellence cannot be achieved by refining or increasing emphasis on the value dimensions of leadership. Excellence requires that the emphasis shift from value to value-added dimensions, and these are cut from a different bolt of cloth.

When shifting the emphasis from value to value-added, sometimes the trick is to build added value to that which already exists. This is the strategy suggested in the four stages of leadership for school improvement discussed and illustrated in Chapter Eight. At other times the initial value dimensions need to be transcended. A good accountability system, for example, is not just built on the process of monitoring but literally transcends the process, making monitoring a needed managerial tool but not the foundation or substance of accountability. To keep things simple, "emphasizing the value-added dimensions" will be used to suggest either a shift in emphasis from one dimension to the other or the transcending of one over the other as appropriate.

Emphasizing Leadership

Few would argue that schools can work well without the presence of competent management, but too often school officials at both state and local levels provide little else. Consequently, too many schools, school districts, and state systems of schooling are over-managed and underled. This condition leads to an undue emphasis on doing things right rather than doing the right things, on following directions rather than solving problems. In searching for the proper balance between management and leadership, H. Ross Perot, the founder of Electronic Data Systems Corporation (EDS), put it this way: "Our country needs strong effective leaders willing to sacrifice to make this country strong. We need to stop managing and start leading" (Shaffer, 1988, p. B8). When head of EDS, Perot operated on the basis of a very simple principle: "People cannot be managed. Inventories can be managed, but people must be led" (Kouzes and Posner, 2003, p. xv). Bob Ansett, former president of Budget Rent-a-Car, Australia, stated: "I probably place more emphasis on Leadership than most company managers, and I do that because I really believe that it is the only way you can establish the right sort of spirit, the commitment that you require, the commitment that is required by a team of people to achieve, and the emphasis on achievement is very high in my organization" (Colin Moyles, undated interview notes. Institute of Educational Leadership. Geelong, Victoria, Australia).

Prior to beginning the research for their landmark book, *In Search of Excellence*, Tom Peters and Robert Waterman (1982) questioned the importance of leadership:

> We must admit that our bias at the beginning was to discount the role of leadership heavily if for no other reason than that everybody's answer to what's "wrong" or "right" with whatever organization is its leader. Our strong belief was that the excellent companies had gotten to be the way they were because of a unique set of

cultural attributes that distinguish them from the rest, and if we understand those attributes well enough, we could do more than just mutter "leadership" in response to questions like "why is J and J so good?" Unfortunately, what we found was that associated with almost every excellent company was a strong leader (or two) who seemed to have had a lot to do with making the company excellent in the first place [p. 26].

Unfortunately, ingrained school bureaucracy and highly prescriptive state regulations often prevent principals and superintendents from exercising the leadership that is needed. This is why Xerox Corporation's former CEO David T. Kearns (1988) argued schools need to be reorganized in such a way that no one but the school superintendent be paid more than the school principal; that central office staff become staff to principals in a system of site-based management rather than another layer of management to which schools must report. Extending his argument, one could reason that state departments of education should be slimmed down similarly and that their responsibilities be changed from trying to run the schools from afar to setting standards, evaluating standards, and providing help to local schools where needed. Many states are now adopting this empowering and supportive role. The result is allowing superintendents, principals, and teachers to provide the needed leadership—at least over the means to achieve ends if not the ends themselves.

The views of corporate leaders are highlighted in this discussion to point out that the need for leadership to be emphasized over management is not a partisan issue put forth by a self-indulgent member of the educational establishment but a necessity if we aspire to quality schooling. Numerous studies of successful schools point to the same conclusion. No matter how competently managed a school may be, it is the extra quality of leadership that makes the difference between ordinary and extra-ordinary performance.

Emphasizing the Performance Investment

A basic principle in work motivation theory and practice is that people invest in work to obtain desired returns or rewards. What is not understood by many who seek to improve our schools is that two very different investments are at stake, each linked to a very different set of returns and rewards—the participation investment and the performance investment. When teachers and principals make the participation investment they meet minimum contractual requirements—they give a fair day's work for a fair day's pay. This is the traditional legal work relationship between employer and employee. But no great institutions in our society and no great achievements have resulted from merely giving a fair day's work for a fair day's pay. Greatness has always been a result of employers and employees exceeding the limits of this relationship.

The performance investment, by contrast, exceeds the limits of the traditional work relationship. Teachers and principals give more than one can reasonably expect. The rewards associated with the participation investment are extrinsic in nature. Teachers, for example, are provided with such benefits as salary, retirement provisions, fair supervision, good human relationships, and security. These are the things that they can reasonably expect as the employing institution meets its basic commitments to its workers. The performance investment, by contrast, is induced by opportunities to experience deep satisfaction with one's work. This reward structure is decidedly more intrinsic.

Emphasizing Symbols and Meaning

In traditional management, school administrators are encouraged to practice situational leadership, carefully calculating behaviors and strategies in a manner that reflects the characteristics of the situations they face and the psychological needs of the people with whom they need to work. There is value in situational leadership and it should be practiced. But in many schools too much attention is given to the instrumental and behavioral aspects of school leadership and life and not enough to the symbolic and cultural aspects. This attention is driven by a behavioristic view of the world. Greatness cannot be tapped, inspired, or enhanced by management practices that emerge from this tradition.

The philosopher Susanne K. Langer reminds us, "Symbols and meaning make man's world, far more than sensation" (1978, p. 28). The author Thomas Carlyle (1937) notes, "It is in and through symbols that man consciously or unconsciously, lives, works, and has his being" (p. 222). By its very nature the human species engages in and thrives on the construction of meaning. Indeed, life's quest is basically the search for meaning. Leadership that counts provides symbols that count and these in turn help humankind in its quest for meaning. As James Quinn (1981) points out, "The role of the leader . . . is one of orchestrator and labeler: taking what can be gotten in the way of action and shaping it—generally after the fact—into lasting commitment to a new strategic direction. In short, he makes meanings" (p. 59). The educational administration theorist Thomas B. Greenfield stated, "The task of leadership is to create the moral order that binds [leaders] and the people around them" (1984, p. viii). When leaders seek to add value to their situational leadership practice, they emphasize symbols and meaning.

Emphasizing Purposing

The concept of vision gets a great deal of play in the leadership literature. In his study of successful leaders, Warren Bennis found vision to be critical. His leaders had "the capacity to create and communicate a compelling vision of a desired state of affairs, a vision that clarifies the current situation and induces commitment to the future" (1984, p. 66; see also Bennis and Nanus, 1985). Vision is important and valuable. Indeed, leaders who are remiss in expressing and articulating a vision, in communicating values and dreams they hold dear, miss the very point of leadership for the school. However, the vision of a school must reflect the hopes and dreams, the needs and interests, and the values and beliefs of teachers, parents, and students as well. In the final analysis it doesn't matter so much what the principal believes; it is what the school stands for that counts.

Effective Visions Are Useful and Are Preceded by Trust

It does not matter how spirited a vision is unless this vision is accompanied by specific commitments that constituents make to bring vision and reality closer together. Effective visions are accompanied by action statements. Visions, as argued in Chapter Three, need to be useful to be effective. Further, as provided in Chapter Four, effective visions are preceded by trust. It is trust first, followed by vision, strategy, and action, that works for serious and long-lasting change to occur. In subsequent chapters, I use the Samuel Gompers Elementary School in Detroit and the Adlai Stevenson High School in Lincolnshire, Illinois, as examples of schools that have gotten the "vision thing" right. In Chapter Eight, I point out that although visionary leaders are important, it is the craftsman archetype of leadership that makes the world go around. Craftsman leaders are good at transforming visions into actions and marshaling the human resources needed for the actions to be successful.

The key to successful schooling is building a covenant comprising purposes and beliefs that bonds people together around common themes and that provides them with a sense of what is important, a signal of what is of value. A covenant is a binding and solemn agreement by principals, teachers, parents, and students to honor certain values, goals, and beliefs; to make certain commitments to each other; and to do or keep from doing specific things. It is the compact that provides the school with a sense of direction on one hand and an opportunity to find meaning in school life on the other. Value-added leaders bring to the school a vision but focus on the building of a shared covenant. The two together make up the leadership dimension of purposing. And purposing is key to helping schools become communities of responsibility.

Emphasizing Enabling of Teachers and the School

In July 1986 the Education Commission of the States issued a report entitled *What Next? More Leverage for Teachers*. In that report Bernard Gifford, then dean of the School of Education at the University of California, Berkeley, stated, "If we are ever going to make a dent in the problems we face in public education, we're going to have to find ways of permitting talented teachers to play a much larger role. We need to find ways of giving talented people, first-rate professionals, extra leverage" (Green, 1986, p. v). This report, along with others issued by the Carnegie Forum (1986), the National Governors Association (1986), the Brackenridge Forum for the Enhancement of Teaching (1987), and dozens of other groups interested in quality schooling, represented a significant turn in America's school reform policy. The key to making things better is to enable teachers—to give them the discretion, the support, the preparation, and the guidance necessary to get the job done.

Enabling teachers is an important aspect of value-added leadership; but more important than teacher empowerment, or for that matter than enabling principals or any other specific group, is enabling the school. It is principals, teachers, parents, and students together who will make the difference in the struggle for building quality schools.

Value-added leaders do not fall into the trap of equating enabling and empowerment with laissez-faire management. Whenever one speaks of enabling, the key question that must be answered is, Enabled to do what? Enabling strategies make sense only when they are linked to the purposes and the requirements for teaching and learning that are implied when a shared covenant emerges in a school. The following "rule" applies: "Principals and teachers are free to do the things that make sense to them providing that the decisions they make embody the shared values and requirements for teaching and learning that comprise the school's covenant." Schools need to be linked similarly to districts, and districts to states, as part of a larger covenant that defines values that are shared by more extended communities. Enabling and empowerment have less to do with rights and more to do with responsibilities. Placing the major emphasis on the school site links rights and responsibilities together firmly.

Emphasizing Accountability

The public cannot have it both ways. Politicians and legislators, school boards and school administrators cannot prescribe in detail what it is that teachers and principals are to do and how they are to do it on one hand and then hold them accountable on the other. In some states, for example, well-intentioned reformers have provided the schools with regulations and requirements that are so detailed that very few decisions are made by principals and teachers about what to teach, when, and how. During his years at the RAND Corporation, Arthur Wise (1979) pointed out that trying to run the affairs of schools by remote control results in legislated learning and in bureaucratic teaching and administration. Academic excellence always suffers under these conditions; standardization is the great friend of mediocrity but the enemy of imagination and excellence. Furthermore, legislated learning and bureaucratic teaching make it impossible to hold individual teachers and principals and individual school communities accountable. They can only be held account-able for results when they have the responsibility for deciding the means and the responsibility for helping to shape the ends.

Monitoring teacher performance and monitoring school perfor-mance are not substitutes for true accountability but only processes that are subsumed under accountability. Understood in this light, monitoring has value. In value-added leadership, monitoring is tran-scended in favor of true accountability.

Emphasizing Intrinsic Motivation

Traditional management theory is based on the principle "what gets rewarded gets done." It makes sense to base motivational strategies and practices on this principle; but when this principle becomes the overriding framework for making decisions about how to lead and how to encourage and reward good performance, the result is the opposite of what is anticipated. In the long run, the job just doesn't get done. The problem with "what gets rewarded gets done" is that it results in calculated involvement of people with their work. When rewards can no longer be provided, the work no longer will be done. Work performance becomes contingent upon a bartering arrangement rather than being self-sustaining because of moral principle or a deeper psychological connection. A better strategy upon which to base our efforts is "what is rewarding gets done." When something is rewarding it gets done even when no one is looking; it gets done even when extrinsic rewards and incentives are scarce or nonexistent; it gets done not because somebody is going to get something in return for it but because it's important. The power of intrinsic motivation is well documented in both research and practice and is a key element in value-added leadership.

Since *Value-Added Leadership* was first published in 1990, I have come to realize that there are three, not two, motivation rules, as follows:

Rule	Motivation	Involvement
1. What gets rewarded gets done	Extrinsic gain	Calculated
2. What is rewarding gets done	Intrinsic gain	Intrinsic
3. What is good gets done	Duty or obligation	Moral

The third rule notes that we are also motivated by duty. What we believe in and what we feel obligated to do because of moral commitments gets done, gets done well, gets done when no one is looking, and gets done even though it might not be extrinsically or intrinsically satisfying to do it. This is the rule that strengthens the heartbeat of leadership and the heartbeat of schools.

Emphasizing Collegiality

Traditional management practices are based on such ideas as POSDCoRB (planning, organizing, staffing, directing, coordinating, reporting, and budgeting), unity of command, "if you can't measure it you can't manage it," regulating the workflow, monitoring, and so on. These ideas are designed to provide a rational system that provides workers with directions as to what to do and controls to ensure that these directions are followed. A cousin to these traditional management ideas is the "Mary Poppins" principle. Because most people don't like to be managed in this way, it becomes necessary to provide "a spoonful of sugar" to help wash this unpleasantness down. For this reason human relations management is not an alternative to traditional management but its country cousin. As enterprises are managed traditionally, it is necessary to work to ensure that morale is kept up.

The emphasis on human relations management has resulted in the value of congeniality becoming very strong in the way schools are managed and led. Congeniality has to do with the climate of interpersonal relationships in an enterprise. When this climate is friendly, agreeable, and sympathetic, congeniality is high. Though congeniality is pleasant and often desirable, it is not *independently* linked to better performance and quality schooling.

For example, in the Organizational Climate Description Questionnaire studies that were popular in the 1960s it was found that congeniality was high in both "open" and "closed" schools (Halpin, 1966). Congeniality can work positively in one school but negatively in another. It all depends on whether the foundation for friendship, agreeableness, and sympathetic understanding comprises values and beliefs that are aligned with quality schooling or values and beliefs that compete with quality schooling. For this reason value-added leaders understand that congeniality alone misses the point (Barth, 1989, p. 230).

Collegiality has to do with the extent to which teachers and principals share common work values, engage in specific conversation about their work, and help each other engage in the work of the school (Little, 1981). Value-added leadership views congeniality as a by-product of building strong collegiality norms in the school and not as an end in itself.

Since *Value-Added Leadership* was published in 1990, I have learned that collegiality alone is not enough to take care of the relationship needs and the learning needs of schools. Teachers and principals, for example, need to be involved in a shared practice for which all are responsible. At its best, this distributing of responsibility across many people resembles a community of practice within which teaching, leading, and learning are thought of as a single practice shared by many. Thus there are three levels of cooperation in a school: congeniality, collegiality, and community of practice. In value-added leadership, communities of practice are the most important. How communities of practice work to bring people together, to build their capacity, and to improve their effectiveness in teaching and learning is described in Chapter Six. Communities of practice, I note, bubble up from teachers to join collaborative cultures that trickle down from designated leaders. Without this blending of the two, efforts of designated leaders are likely to lead to contrived collegiality.

Emphasizing Leadership by Outrage

Is it important for students to come to school? Wilma Parrish, the principal of Western Middle School in Alamance County, North Carolina, thought so. She was known to drive to absent students' houses to find out why they missed and on occasion to drag them back to school. It should come as no surprise that attendance at Western rose to about 98 percent. Wilma Parrish was a remarkable principal with a nose for quality and a determination to succeed; and when things were not right she was quick to get them fixed. Joan Lipsitz studied the Western Middle School as part of her research on successful schools. She described Wilma Parrish as a person ahead of and behind her teachers, constantly leading and prodding. She had high expectations for teachers and communicated them clearly. As Lipsitz notes,

> The significantly less dedicated of her classroom teachers have come to know the results of not meeting her standards. In such cases, RIF [reduced in force] probationary teachers stay RIF, and tenured but inadequate teachers know that tenured means exactly what it is legally supposed to mean: they will be fairly evaluated and then dismissed through proper due process. In one instance, a tenured teacher resigned because the pressure from Mrs. Parrish to perform became too great, the rewards too few. In another instance, a teacher with twenty-three years' experience who had become incompetent was fired. One way or another, the message from the principal to achieve excellence in the classroom is clear [Lipsitz, 1984, p. 35].

Wilma Parrish practiced leadership by outrage. Despite standard prescriptions in the management literature that admonish leaders to be cool, calculated, and reserved in all that they say or do, she brought to her practice a sense of passion and risk that communicated to others that if something was worth believing in then it was worth showing passion over. In his extensive studies of successful leaders, Peter Vaill (1984) found that their leadership practice was characterized by time, feeling, and focus. Leaders put in extraordinary amounts of time, had very strong feelings about the attainment of the system's purpose, and focused on key issues and variables. Key in his analysis of this time-feeling-focus triad is the importance of *feeling* in linking together the other two. He found that successful leaders care deeply about the system, its purposes, structure, conduct, history, future security, and underlying values and commitments. They care deeply enough to show passion, and when things are not going right this passion often takes the form of outrage.

Leadership by outrage is a symbolic act that communicates importance and meaning and touches people in ways not possible when leadership is viewed entirely as something objective and calculated. For this reason its use over issues of purpose defined by the school's shared covenant adds value to leadership.

The Dimensions Together

None of the dimensions of value-added leadership, considered alone, is powerful enough to make the difference in bringing about quality education in America. Indeed a critical connectedness exists among the characteristics and dimensions, and value-added leadership is best understood as comprising interdependent parts. Practicing enabling leadership, for example, without practicing leadership that emphasizes purposing and the building of a covenant is more likely to result in laissez-faire management than in quality schooling. Furthermore, emphasizing management at the expense of leadership— by providing controls and regulations, by emphasizing authority, by attempting to regulate the flow and work of schooling—will not allow the practice of convincing and meaningful empowerment. A school that builds a covenant comprising technical statements of objectives, targets, and outcomes that fail to inspire, that are devoid of symbolic representations, and that do not allow principals, parents, teachers, and students to derive sense and meaning from their school lives will fail.

In his address "The Four Simple Truths of Management," Donald M. Kendall (1986), former CEO of PepsiCo Inc., illustrated the interdependent nature of value-added leadership dimensions. The "truths" he offered are as follows: Complex organizations are best managed on a decentralized basis. However, decentralization only works when there is a central purpose to the entire organization— "a central plan against which all the separate elements can be gauged. But the development of specific objectives that support this central plan—and the development of the specific strategies, products and programs—these are the responsibility of the operating units" (p. 476). Kendall believed that it is important to give people "the freedom to operate within broad guidelines, not within the narrow confines of a detailed program dictated by top management. . . . The job of senior management, then, is to measure results, monitor progress and help the operating people take corrective action wherever necessary" (p. 476).

Kendall's linchpin for keeping everything together in a nonbureaucratic organization is top management's ability "to create a vision of the organization, a sense of purpose." He adds, "Everyone knows what it was that made the organization successful in the past, and what it will take to ensure the continuation of that success" (p. 477). This covenant needs to provide meaning to those in the organization. "All of us want meaning in our lives beyond a paycheck, beyond daily sustenance, we want the opportunity to share great values and great visions—and to have a real part of turning these values and visions into reality" (p. 477).

I have since learned that the key to running a successful school depends on its ability to transform vision into reality and that it is the craftsman leaders who have the dispositions, know-how, and skill to get this done. Emphasizing leadership, symbols and meaning, the building of a shared covenant, and school site empowerment and accountability, therefore, are a package deal. When intrinsic motivation, moral obligation, collegiality, communities of practice, and leadership by outrage are added to this package we have value-added leadership in action.

Corollary 1: Building in Canvas

In describing the difference between administrative theory and administrative life, the noted organizational theorist James G. March (1984) stated, "The way we talk may sometimes be less sensible than our administrative behavior—the way we act" (p. 19). As successful leaders have come to learn, the talk of administration is the way one gets legitimacy; and legitimacy, in turn, gives one freedom to act. The action of administration is the way one gets results. Schools and other organizations in our society operate in an open environment within which they are expected to respond to the images and expectations of sponsors. If they are successful, sponsors provide the needed support for them to function and the needed discretion to function freely. Schools, for example, are sponsored by powerful state bureaucracies that provide a host of expectations that they operate in bureaucratic ways. Papers must be filed, data must be accumulated, teachers must be evaluated according to rules, schedules must be followed, and so on. These bureaucratic values are sometimes reinforced by rule-happy and top-heavy local school districts' central offices. If local school leaders follow these rules to the letter, excellence remains out of reach and basic competence is endangered. If they do not follow these rules, they might find themselves in trouble at the hands of a vindictive bureaucracy.

The challenge is to reflect the images and values of bureaucratic sponsors on one hand and to make the decisions that count for excellence in schools on the other. The answer is to build bureaucratic systems in canvas—like the folding canvas tanks the U.S. military built to serve as decoys while creating an illusion of strength. Building in canvas is not a bad idea when tinkering with the structure of schooling.

Schools have multiple and often conflicting purposes that make exact alignment of structure and purpose difficult, if not impossible. In the real world schools must look the way they are supposed to. To obtain legitimacy the school must be able to communicate to its sponsors a feeling of competence. In return it receives needed statements of confidence. Because of their relative remoteness, bureaucratic sponsors are attracted to the general features of school structure rather than to the details of how these features are being interpreted in day-to-day schooling. Therefore, schools have a surprising amount of freedom as they interpret policies and rules in ways that support sensible teaching and learning.

If schools master the art of building in canvas, they are able to provide the right public face—thus gaining the freedom to interpret, decide, and function in ways that make more sense for teaching and learning.

Corollary 2: Emphasizing Moral Leadership

Creating illusions and building in canvas raise obvious moral questions in the minds of many. Some might argue that such ideas are deceptive and have no place in the lexicon of leadership. Moral questions, however, are not raised when school leaders are being sensitive to such human realities as the loose connectedness of school parts, the competing preferences and interests of the school community, the need for people to construct their own reality, and the importance of norms and values. Instead moral questions are raised when school leaders ignore these realities by continuing to push ill-fitting management theories. The result is an attempt to shape human nature to fit theory. A moral approach would be to use a theory that fits people better in the first place as the basis for school improvement.

Not only must management and leadership theory fit human nature, it must enhance teaching and learning and other dimensions of the school's covenant as well. Bureaucratic theories of leadership are secular. They seek a response from the human mind and hand. But the unique human response is one of spirit, and the spirit responds to values, beliefs, moral dimensions, and standards. Moral leadership taps the spirit. How credible is the leader? Is the leader honest, forthright, and sincere? Does the leader model beliefs, live purposes, exemplify standards? In essence, what does the leader represent, and does this representation symbolize something of value to followers? In value-added leadership authority takes on moral characteristics.

Moral questions about leadership are unavoidable. Whenever there is an unequal distribution of power between two people, the relationship becomes a moral one. Leadership involves an offer to control. The follower accepts this offer on the assumption that control will not be exploited. In this sense leadership is a responsibility. Its purpose is not to enhance the leader but to enhance the school. Leaders minister to the needs of the school by being of service and by providing help. The test of moral leadership is whether the competence, well-being, and independence of the follower is enhanced as a result of accepting control and whether the enterprise of which both are a part ultimately benefits. In schools that means teaching and learning are enhanced and the developmental needs of students are honored.

Leadership combines management know-how with values and ethics. Leadership practice, as a result, is always concerned with both what is effective and what is good; what works and what makes sense; doing things right and doing right things. As school-improvement projects are considered, questions of what is good, what makes sense, and what is worth doing deserve equal billing with questions of effectiveness and efficiency. When the two sides of the ledger are in conflict, leaders will be known by the side they emphasize. For these reasons moral considerations are both the beginning and the end of value-added leadership. The governing rule for the practice of value-added leadership comes from Kant ([1785] 1959): "Act so that you treat humanity, whether in your own person or in that of another, always as an end and never as a means only" (p. 47).

1

Mindscapes

A strong heartbeat is a school's best defense against the obstacles leaders face as they work to change schools for the better. But strengthening the heartbeat of a school requires that we rethink what leadership is, how leadership works, what leadership's relationship to learning is, and why we need to practice both leadership and learning together.

When leaders are able to strengthen the heartbeat, their schools become stronger and more resilient. These qualities help leaders to share the burdens of leadership with others, to create collaborative cultures, and to be continuous learners. Leadership inevitably involves change and change inevitably involves learning. Both are easier to do the better we understand the mindscapes we bring to our practice, examine them in light of what we want to do, and change them. Change begins with us—with our heart, our head, and our hands that drive our leadership practice.

Lots of words could be used to capture the meaning of *heartbeat*. Three cousins—*social capital, community,* and *relational trust*—are good examples. Each of the cousins is a little different. Social capital provides the support students and teachers need (Coleman, 1988). Community provides the caring that students and teachers need (Sergiovanni, 1994). And relational trust provides the basis for developing deep reciprocal roles and role relationships with strong moral overtones (Bryk and Schneider, 2002). Reciprocal roles and role relationships can transform schools from ordinary to sacred places. They are essential, for example, in building community in schools. Taken together the three cousins enrich leadership and show how a strengthened school heartbeat can provide support for deep learning for both teachers and students.

Conventional wisdom tells us that leadership is about finding solutions to the problems that people face. But in reality leadership is more about helping people gain an understanding of problems they face and about helping them manage these problems and even learn to live with them. Even in the best of circumstances leadership is not easy. Community is a good example. Few leaders find their efforts at community building to be models of perfect harmony. Important differences exist among any faculty that is alive and well. But the wise leader knows that schools need centers of harmony that contain enough of what is important and shared to hold things together. At the same time they encourage differences in how this center of ideas is embodied in practice. Community for them is like a mosaic (see, for example, Etzioni 1996/1997) composed of many different elements held together by a common frame and glue.

Few leaders have all the competence, all the time, and all the information needed at any one time to get the job done. The wise among them try hard to rely on others and to build up the leadership capacity in others. Leaders have funds of knowledge and funds of skills that need constant replenishment. An important part of their job is to cultivate and amass the intellectual capital needed for the school's organizational I.Q. to increase. No doubt smart leaders help, but it is smart schools that will make the difference over time. That is why leadership and learning together are so important. We can have leadership and we can have learning. We can focus on individuals and we can focus on the school. We can view learning as a private good that serves individual interests but has little to do with pursuing school goals. And we can view learning as something individuals feel compelled to do because it is a public good that helps schools achieve their goals (Elmore, 2002). In each case effects multiply when these dimensions are brought together.

Head, Heart, and Hand

When we talk about and write about leadership, we usually emphasize the hand of leadership—the actions and behaviors that leaders
use. Sometimes we include the problems that leaders face as they
practice and the obstacles that keep them from behaving the way
they want to. A popular theme of researchers is to gauge the success or failure of leaders and then to identify the behaviors and
actions that seem to be causing these effects. These are important
concerns and important issues that make describing and understanding the hand of leadership valuable. But we can't stop here.
The hand alone is not powerful enough to account for what leadership is; indeed, the hand may not represent leadership at all. If we
want to understand a leader's behavior, we have to examine the
heart and the head of leadership too.

Both the heart and head of leadership function as mindscapes.
The heart has to do with what a person believes, values, hopes for,
and is committed to—a person's personal vision, to use the popular
term. But it is more than vision. It is a whole interior world, which
becomes the foundation of that person's reality. At the school level,
the heart of leadership is much like a school's repository of values,
assumptions, and beliefs that are widely shared and that serve as a
source of authority for what people do. The values, assumptions,
and beliefs of the heart also create realities and define truths as they
become an important part of a school's shared mindscape—the ever
important center that holds things together. "The center . . . is a
phenomenon of the realm of values and beliefs . . . which govern
the society. . . . In a sense, society has an official 'religion'. . . . The
center is also a phenomenon of the realm of action. It is a structure
of activities, of roles and persons, within the network of institutions.
It is in these that the values and beliefs which are central are
embodied and propounded" (Shils, 1961, p. 119).

The head of leadership is a source of mindscapes themed to the
theories of teaching and learning, the theories of organization and
management, and the theories of people that are adopted and then

govern the collective behavior of teachers, students, and others. Once these mindscapes from the head are shared, they begin to program the minds of people in such a way that a collective image of reality is created. This reality can provide the instructional coherence, the organizational coherence, and the leadership coherence that schools need to succeed.

From Mindscapes to Action

Shared mindscapes also provide the context for the expression of leadership:

- The heart of leadership: What do we value?

- The head of leadership: What are our theories?

- The hand of leadership: How do we behave?

Differences are always a part of this sharing. But to qualify as a shared mindscape, differences must be muted by core purposes, values, and ideas. I've written on this at length in the past:

> Mindscapes are implicit mental frames through which . . . reality and our place in this reality are envisioned. Mindscapes provide us with intellectual and psychological images of the real world and the boundaries and parameters of rationality that help us to make sense of this world. In a very special way, mindscapes are intellectual security blankets on the one hand and road maps through an uncertain world on the other. As road maps they provide the rules, assumptions, images, and practice exemplars that define for us what . . . is [Sergiovanni, 1985, p. 6].

And further,

So complete is the programming of a mindscape that its assumptions and practices are automatically accepted and articulated. Mindscapes are not thought about very much, for they are assumed to be true. Thus when a . . . mindscape does not fit the world of practice, the problem is assumed to be *in that world*. Rarely is the world accepted for what it is and the prevailing mindscapes challenged or indeed abandoned in favor of others [Sergiovanni, 1985, p. 6].

How Mindscapes Work

Normally what we do makes sense to us. Our thoughts and behaviors seem to fit the mindscapes that we have as individuals and that we hold collectively as a school. The school across the street may not understand why we do the things we do. And we are equally mystified by some of their assumptions and practices. This is because our shared mindscapes may differ. But we can't just shrug our shoulders and say that's okay. We can't just adopt an "anything goes" mentality. Not all mindscapes are equally good and not all of the resulting practices are equally right or effective.

All this is complicated by the reality that frequently individuals and schools adopt mindscapes without realizing it. Complicated or not, if we are going to get anywhere in improving schools, individual and collective mindscapes have to be exposed and discussed. And their goodness and effectiveness need to be debated. Researchers seeking "best practices" need to take shared mindscapes into account. Further, both individual and collective mindscapes need to be made explicit. Tacitly held mindscapes at either the individual level or the school level undermine change, make learning difficult, and make the building of collegiality among teachers virtually impossible. If we are going to talk about something in a meaningful way, we have to get our ideas, our values, and our hopes out on the table—and so do others. Once on the table and agreed to, mindscapes can be used as sources of authority for what we do and as benchmarks for evaluating how well we are doing it.

Effective mindscapes are those that include agreed-upon solutions to the core problems a school faces. Agreed-upon solutions lead to predictable behavior. An important caveat is to view these mindscapes as frameworks and statements of values rather than as templates that script everything people must do. A school, for example, might be trying to close the achievement gap among different groups of students. This school is committed to the idea that it must strive to become a culture of learning for students and adults alike. As a result the members of this school believe, "We can close the gap if we pull together and learn together and share what we have learned." One strategy that they adopt is focusing relentlessly on examining student work and on examining the assignments teachers give in light of the standards that they are pursuing. They decide to adopt this strategy because of their firm commitment to underlying values, including the importance of collaboration and the importance of hope, themes I will discuss in Chapter Four. Further, they find validating research that shows that when teachers organize learning around assignments requiring higher-level thinking, understanding, elaborative communications, and the application to student lives, student learning reflects more intellectually complex work. Newmann and his colleagues' studies of the assignments that Chicago teachers give bear out this finding. Students who received assignments requiring more challenging work achieved greater than average gains on the Iowa Test of Basic Skills (Newmann, Bryk, and Nagaoka, 2001).

The key questions members of this school ask are: Is the work that students do up to standards? Do assignments we give require that students work to standards? They hope that this investigation will lead teachers to write lessons that are more on target. Lessons might then be swapped, critiqued, and practice-taught as a way to test their usefulness and their accuracy with respect to the standards. These lessons might then be stored in public files so that all teachers have access to them. These files would contain, as well, comments, evaluations, and suggestions for improvement written by teachers who have used the lesson. Sometimes samples of student work would be clipped to the lessons to show the kind of learning the lessons produced. From time to time the lessons would be reviewed, revised, and even over-hauled. This strategy for pulling together and learning together is predictable given the mindscapes that are at the heart of the culture that this school is trying to create.

Culture

Spindler (1984) writes, "Culture . . . refers to shared designs for liv-ing. It is not the people or things or behavior themselves. Culture can be equated with the *shared models* people carry in their minds for perceiving, relating to, and interpreting the world around them" (pp. 4–5). James March (1984) puts it this way:

> We live by the interpretations we make, become better or worse through the meanings we impute to events and institutions. Our lives change when our beliefs change. Administrators manage the way the sentiments, expec-tations, commitments, and faiths of individuals con-cerned with the organization fit into a structure of social beliefs about organizational life. Administrative theory probably underestimates the significance of this belief structure for effective organizations. As a result, it prob-ably underestimates the extent to which the management of symbols is a part of effective administration [p. 32].

One way to examine prevailing and competing mindscapes is by using metaphors. Metaphors are shortcuts to understanding and are particularly useful for comparing different understandings of the same thing. As Lakoff and Johnson (1980) explain, in the world of metaphors truth is both subjective and objective. Truth is always subjective between conceptual systems and only objective within them. In the section that follows I will use metaphors to show how mindscapes work and to gauge views of important teaching, learning, and school issues—views that will affect how we will lead, why we will lead, and where our leadership will take us.

Exposing Mindscapes

There are risks in exposing mindscapes. Most of us have a great deal invested in the ways we presently do things. The large high school is a good example. Despite the overwhelming amount of research that tells us that by and large small schools are good for students, there is still much resistance. It would be unfair to characterize all high schools the same way or to impute the same motivations to their leaders. Still, principals of large high schools do enjoy considerable prestige— prestige that many find worth protecting. The large middle management teams usually found in large high schools have worked hard to get their jobs and no doubt want to keep them. Some career-bound assistant principals, for example, view their jobs as stepping stones to getting their own principalships. Rarely do they pay attention to the research on school size. Instead, those who want to protect the large high school point to the array of offerings that such a school can provide students, to the belief that large high schools are cost-effective (Gregory, 1992; Sergiovanni, 1996), to the community politics that may arise if changes are made, and to other alleged advantages. Perhaps the words of Carlina Rinaldi can help us think differently:

> Often in our work, and in our lives, we tend to look for
> confirmation of what we think and what we believe. We
> identify our selves with our ideas and our theories. To
> change our minds, to reconsider our basic theories and
> beliefs so as to see their limitations, is often perceived as
> a personal defeat. Often the ensuing crisis is experienced
> as a loss rather than as the beginning of something new.

The fact is that we are too firmly attached to our theories
and to our ideas and thus we often close the door to new
ways of seeing and understanding [Rinaldi, 2003, p. x].

Marching Bands and Soccer Teams

In some ways we take the value of building community in schools
for granted. Everyone seems to say they are for community and the
literature is full of references to schools as communities. Is community worth all the attention it is getting? Do schools really need the
benefits of community to be effective? The answers to these questions depend on your view of the school. Picture, for example, two
metaphors for the school—the marching band and the soccer team.
Within the marching band, school personnel march in unison—
even lockstep—following a carefully prescribed script. The play of
individual players is hidden by the band itself. Once the band begins
its march, changing the route is difficult if not impossible. As it
passes in review the band is judged good or bad according to a formula that examines the precision of the marching and the way
notes are played. But it is hard for viewers to know why a rating is
assigned. As accomplished musicians know, good music is played in
between the lines rather than with the notes themselves.

Still, marching bands that play well have a number of advantages. When everyone plays the same way at the same time they
often create an impressive, even thrilling, performance and make
the bandleader a hero. Given today's school improvement policies,
schools are beginning to look more and more like marching
bands—and as a result, the principal as hero bandleader is becoming
the dominant image for leadership—an image, by the way, that
some principals find attractive. In the past they weren't quite sure
of what to do in the classroom. They weren't quite sure of what this
instructional leadership business was all about and they felt threatened as a result. Now, having been trained to read the band music
in the same way and to read the marching script as well, our hero

bandleaders are able to tell what "good instruction" looks like and, to make things easier, it pretty much looks the same everywhere. They are trained to monitor and evaluate the band to be sure it is doing what it is supposed to do. All they have to do now is to figure out how to get people to follow the right directions and to teach the same things in pretty much the same ways. But scripting the band's performance has its downside too.

We move in cycles in our understanding of school leadership. In the 1980s principals were supposed to be strong instructional leaders who were good at leading the band. During the 1990s principals were thought of as leaders of leaders who were supposed to develop the capacity and will of teachers so that they (the teachers) could be instructional leaders. This was a decade of teacher leadership and teacher quality. Here we are in another decade down the road writing standards for principals and providing principals with training so that they can once again be more effective instructional leaders, able to bring the bands that they lead to new heights of quality.

In the soccer team metaphor schools move more fluidly, making their way toward scoring goals by developing their practice as they go along, and in light of constantly changing streams of action. The game is governed by a few rules and a common framework, but no scripts. Players make lots of decisions on the spot as they evaluate the situations they face. The play of each player is public and accountability is built into the game itself (you can see who is doing what).

In marching bands community doesn't matter all that much. Sure, we can use the language of community to be in vogue—but we don't need community to make our schools work well. Sure, community can help build the band's morale and esprit, but benefits are limited since virtually everything important is decided beforehand. Playing well requires following directions and being in step with those around you.

The soccer team, by contrast, can't play successfully without the benefits of community that reach beyond esprit—benefits that bond players together as they are bound to common commitments so that mentally and physically their play is both flexible and coordinated at the same time. Success depends on the development of communities of learners, communities of practice, and communities of responsibility. These are real communities—not the communities of cheerleaders that march on the sidelines urging the band along.

Community as a Theory of Practice

When we live in a soccer team world we have no choice but to use community as our theory of practice. Why is this the case? Because community provides the glue that holds everything together. In the marching band, by contrast, things are held together by the official script and by the skilled supervision of the bandleader. Community serves the soccer team as a substitute for marching orders, for patterns to produce, and once play is under way even for the bandleader. Community provides the connections that players need for both individual and team play. Leadership from the sidelines counts, but its focus is on helping players become more self-learning, self-managing, and helpful to other players. Rare is the soccer team that does not depend on leadership from its players. Soccer coaches are quick to point out that leadership on the field as the game is actually being played wins games, not leadership on the sidelines or in the locker room.[1]

[1] Jerald Hage and Charles Powers (1992) also use soccer as a metaphor but contrast it with baseball as follows: "Baseball is a highly scripted game. Adjusted responses to unfolding conditions are quite predictable. A person paying attention to the game can confidently predict what every player on the field will do if, for example, a fly ball is hit. Baseball emphasizes learning rules, not being creative. By contrast, it is far more difficult to predict what will happen as the ball goes into play in a game of basketball or soccer. Both are faster moving games that not only allow for more scenarios but also constrain players less in their selection of scenarios. These games require more complex imaginative rehearsal and more fluid adjusted response, and players need better interaction skills in order to accurately read opponents. They are games that offer more room for innovative responses and creativity. Consequently, they more accurately reflect the kinds of lives adults now lead" (pp. 69–70).

Communities share many characteristics (see, for example, Sergiovanni, 1994, 2001). They spring from common understandings that provide members with a sense of identity and involvement that results in the creation of a web of meaningful relationships with moral overtones. Community has many meanings but at root is the Latin *communis* and *communitas*. *Communis* means common, and *communitas* means fellowship. Thus say Carey and Frohnen (1998): "A true community . . . is one in which members share something in common—something important enough to give rise to fellowship . . . and to sustain it. There may be many kinds of communities with varying ends or goals. But each must form around characteristics, experiences, practices, and beliefs that are important enough to bind the members to one another, such that they are willing to sacrifice for one another as 'fellows' or sharers of a common fate" (p. 1–2).

Here is the picture: When people gather together to share ideas and commit themselves to these ideas their relationships change—they have made promises to each other and are likely to feel morally obliged to keep their promises. Communities embody civic virtue—the willingness of people to sacrifice their self-interest on behalf of the common good. And this virtue is the reason why communities can be so powerful in uniting parents, teachers, and students in common purpose. And, if researchers are to be believed, this common purpose provides the focus and the moral commitment that contributes to school effectiveness (see, for example, Bryk and Driscoll, 1988; Hill, Foster, and Gendler, 1990; Hill and Celio, 1998). But none of this community business makes sense if our mindscape is that of the marching band rather than the soccer team.

Management Mindscapes

Traditional management theory is based on a view of how schools operate that does not fit the real world very well. When leadership practices are based on this view they don't work the way they are supposed to. Traditional management assumes that by and large schools are "managerially tight and culturally loose." According to this theory, what counts in improving schools is management of connections, not people. When this is the case, the operation of schools resembles the mechanical workings of a clock—cogs and gears, wheels, drives, and pins, all tightly connected in an orderly and predictable manner. This is the "Clockwork I" theory of management.

Clockwork I school leaders believe that the purpose of leadership is to gain control over what people do and how they do it by regulating the master wheel and the master pin of their clockwork organization. This is sometimes done by introducing such ideas as a highly sequenced curriculum prescribed in excruciating detail, a testing program that narrows what is taught to such an extent that the test alone becomes the curriculum, a supervisory system for monitoring in detail what teachers do and for evaluating their teaching behaviors in a standard way, or a program that trains teachers to implement a specific teaching model thought to represent the "one best way." Such highly refined and hyper-rational management systems are introduced to ensure that teachers will teach the way they are supposed to and students will be taught what they are supposed to learn. Unfortunately this rarely happens—at least not on a sustained and continuous basis and not without excessive monitoring and other enforcement efforts. When such a system does work, it gets people to do what they are supposed to but not more.

In 1976, the noted social psychologist Karl Weick wrote a seminal article for the *Administrative Science Quarterly* describing educational organizations as "loosely coupled systems." His metaphor complements the work of Stanford University's James G. March, who is recognized as one of America's most eminent organizational scientists. March and a number of his colleagues have written extensively on the extent to which educational organizations resemble organized anarchies and on the link between ambiguity and leadership (March and Olsen, 1976). These are concepts similar to loose coupling. Weick pointed out that in schools each of the parts that make up the whole are only loosely connected. What happens in one place seems to have little effect on what happens elsewhere. For example, a good deal of time and effort is spent in schools on developing curriculum. The curriculum that gets taught, however, tends not to be this official curriculum but the one that is in the minds and hearts of teachers. Administrators spend a good deal of time writing memos that are not read or that when read are often ignored. Models of teaching are adopted but don't find their way into the classroom on a sustained basis without constant monitoring.

Weick's observations and those of March provide an image of schools that function like a clockwork gone awry. We might refer to this image as the "Clockwork II" theory of management—a theory of cogs, gears, and pins all spinning independently of each other. The question is, of course, How does a leader bring about the needed coherence for schools to function in a sensible way? Using such control techniques as going for the main gear and pin as a management strategy just doesn't work, since the gears and pins are not tightly connected to each other or to any of the other parts. Instead the leader must rely on "cultural cement" to provide the necessary connections for coordination and control. The ingredients for cultural cement are the norms, values, beliefs, and purposes of people. Weick (1982) advises school leaders to "be attentive to the 'glue' that holds loosely coupled systems together because such forms are just barely systems" (p. 675). March (1984) similarly advises, "If we want to identify one single way in which administrators can affect organizations, it is through their effect on the worldviews that surround organizational life; those effects are managed through attention to the ritual and symbolic characteristics of organizations and their administration. Whether we wish to sustain the system or change it, management is a way of making a symbolic statement" (p. 32).

Instructional Coherence

No doubt a certain amount of standardization is unavoidable and even desirable. Newmann, Smith, Allensworth, and Bryk (2001), for example, found "a strong positive relationship between improving coherence and improving student achievement" (p. 305). They define instructional coherence as "a set of interrelated programs for students and staff that are guided by a common framework for curriculum, instruction, assessment, and learning climate and that are pursued over a sustained period" (p. 297). But there are vast differences between standardizing strategies that seek instructional and other kinds of coherence and hyper-rationality. State-mandated teacher evaluation systems that rely on lengthy lists of teaching behaviors that must be demonstrated by the teacher under observation are an example. By and large teachers willingly showboat required behaviors when they are being observed. However, the question for anyone concerned with wise use of taxpayers' dollars and genuine school improvement is what happens when the evaluators are not there. As you can imagine, when no one is looking teachers teach in ways that make sense to them. Unfortunately for the Clockwork I thinkers the average elementary school teacher teaches about sixteen hundred lessons a year. Spending millions of dollars to be sure at least two or three of those lessons were done in a particular way just doesn't make sense.

Despite the fact that policies and practices based on Clockwork I theory are costly and ineffectual, they persist because they provide the illusion of success. Too often politicians and bureaucrats settle for this illusion. If teachers are being vigorously evaluated, then presumably teaching must be getting better. Rarely, however, does one hear of a teacher getting fired as a result of being evaluated by a Clockwork I system. As Newmann, Smith, Allensworth, and Bryk (2001) point out, "Strong school-level leadership is central to the development of stronger instructional program coherence, but coherence achieved by administrative fiat is of questionable value when it suppresses the development of equally essential supports for learning, such as teachers' professional community and shared ownership of an instructional program" (p. 311). Perhaps the answer is finding the right balance between a bureaucratic version of coherence that relies on *control* and a more professional version of coherence that relies on *commitment* (Rowan, 1990). But this balance cannot be an arbitrary cut of a deck of cards. A school's coherence strategy needs to have a clear identity and must be implemented with gusto if it is to work. The heartbeat of a school is strongest when commitment strategies are at the center and control strategies are at the periphery. Control strategies help ensure that the routines of learning get deliberate and systematic attention, while commitment strategies help ensure that authentic learning content and processes are mastered.

In sum, advocates of the Clockwork II theory argue that schools should not be viewed as managerially tight and culturally loose but as managerially loose and culturally tight. What matters most, they say, is not management connections but the beliefs, values, and norms that hold people together. Failure to recognize this inverse rule leads to the development of policies and school improvement strategies that are costly, inefficient, and ineffective.

Theories of Rationality

The mindscapes we hold about rationality are seminal to the development of our worldviews and foundational to our leadership practice. More often than not when competing views of educational issues and practices are debated it is because of different mindscapes that are creating differing realities, which in turn lead to different policies and to different practices.

When a school leader chooses a theory from which to practice, a particular image of rationality is assumed—whether or not it fits the real world. A better fit between theory and practice will occur by starting the other way around. Choose the image of rationality that fits the real world first and then find a theory that fits that image of rationality.

Lee Shulman (1989, p. 171) provides three mindscapes of human rationality, each described briefly here. The following descriptions are slightly edited but essentially in Shulman's words. All three are true to a certain extent, but some are more true than others. It makes a difference which of the three or which combination of the three provides the strategic basis for one's leadership practice. Using a maximum of ten points, distribute the points across the three to reflect the extent to which you think each is true. If you think that #2 is not true but #1 and #3 are equally true, assign five points to 1 and 3 and no points to 2. Divide your points equally if you feel that each of the three is equally true.

1. *Humans are rational;* they think and act in a manner consistent with their goals, their self-interest, and what they have been rewarded for. If you wish them to behave in a given way, make the desired behavior clear to them and make it worth their while to engage in it.

2. *Humans are limited in their rationality;* they can make sense of only a small piece of the world at a time and they strive to act reasonably with respect to their limited grasp of facts and alternatives. They must, therefore, construct conceptions or definitions of situations rather than passively accept what is presented to them. If you wish them to change, engage them in active problem solving and judgment, don't just tell them what to do.

3. *Humans are rational only when acting together;* since individual reason is so limited, men and women find opportunities to work jointly on important problems, achieving through joint effort what individual reason and capacity could never accomplish. If you want them to change, develop ways in which they can engage in the change process jointly with peers.

The first mindscape of human rationality fits traditional management theories very well. The second and third mindscapes, by contrast, are better accommodated by the Clockwork II theory of management and a value-added approach to leadership. Within the second and third, rationality is achieved by helping people make sense of their world. As making sense builds, limits on rationality are overcome. The ability to make sense builds when people are able to construct their own definitions of situations and are involved with the leader in active problem solving. The limits, however, are too great for anyone to do it alone. Thus one key strategy for sense building is the pooling of human resources and the fostering of collegial values in an effort that expands individual reason and capacity to function. Linda Lambert's definition of constructivist leadership fits well here. To her, leadership is a reciprocal process that enables people to construct meanings that lead to shared purposes of schools (Lambert and others, 2002, p. 42).

Leadership and Rationality

When exercising leadership in accordance with the first view of rationality the leader emphasizes, in order, ends, ways, and means. First establish your objectives. Then, given your objectives, develop a plan that includes the proper management protocols for obtaining goals. These protocols should help figure out the best ways, the clearest paths that will logically and effectively lead to your ends. Next marshal your human resources. Figure out how you're going to orient, direct, train, motivate, and monitor them so that they follow the right paths. Provide the necessary expectations and the psychological support that will allow them to undertake their assigned responsibilities with ease. Ends-ways-means assumes a certain predictability, stability, and rationality that often does not exist in the real world. It fits, for example, a world that is always managerially tight and culturally loose; but when the world is managerially loose and culturally tight, ends-ways-means does not work well. Furthermore, this view of planning places too much of the burden for school success on the principal or the designated leader. It becomes the leader's job to set the system up, to command compliance, and to provide the necessary controls to ensure compliance.

In a managerially loose and culturally tight world one needs to plan in reverse. Ends-ways-means must become means-ways-ends. Planning in reverse is consistent with the second and third mindscapes of rationality. Without losing sight of the overall vision the leader first emphasizes means, then moves to ways, and finally to ends. As Harvard Business School professor Robert H. Hayes (1985) points out, "An organization that takes a means-ways-ends approach to strategic planning assumes everybody is responsible for its prosperity. Its success rests on its ability to exploit opportunities as they arise, on its ingenuity and on its capacity to learn, on its determination and persistence" (p. 118). When planning in reverse the emphasis is on development of people, on building their talents and commitments, on linking them to colleagues so that together they are able to accomplish more, on encouraging their minds and hearts, and helping their hands. Once human resources are built up in both skill and heart, then the school is better able to acquire and develop new and better ways to function, to create opportunities, and to exploit circumstances in a manner that results in more effective school performance. Because of the unpredictability of the world and the limits of human rationality, it makes sense to emphasize building capabilities of people and then to encourage *them* to develop the ways and means for using their capabilities. Developing detailed plans first and then seeking the know-how and commitment from people to implement these plans will not work as well.

Planning in reverse is consistent with the second and third mindscapes of rationality. In my experience, both second and third views come close to the heartbeat of leadership and to the heartbeat of a school, and both provide an important source of authority for principals, teachers, and others to lead and learn together. What about you? How did you distribute your points across the three? What are the reasons for your distribution? Can you recall instances from your experience that matched your distribution of points?

Know Thyself

You get what you see, you see what you expect, and you expect what you believe to be true. Karl Weick tells the story (cited in Mintzberg, Ahlstrand, and Lampel, 1998, pp. 159–160) of a military unit on maneuvers in the Alps that failed to return to base after two days in a snowstorm. On the third day the soldiers appeared. "Yes, they said, we considered ourselves lost and waited for the end. And one of us found a map in his pocket. That calmed us down. We pitched camp, lasted out the snowstorm, and through the map we discovered our bearings. And here we are. The lieutenant [who had dispatched the unit] borrowed this remarkable map and had a good look at it. He discovered to his astonishment that it was not a map of the Alps, but a map of the Pyrenees." As Weick explains, "With the map in hand, no matter how crude it is, people encode what they see to conform as closely as possible to what is on the map. The map prefigures their perceptions, and they see what they expect to see. But, as discrepancies accumulate, they pay closer attention to what is in their immediate experience, look for patterns in it, and pay less attention to the map."

Mindscapes operate a lot like maps. They shape our perceptions and we see what we expect to see. Mindscapes also have a stealth quality to them. Unnoticed, they frame the way we think and then provide us with a rationale for legitimizing our thoughts and actions. They work unknowingly and are difficult to escape from. Figuring out ways to help leaders break out is an important step in bringing about change. By paying attention to mindscapes and by knowing ourselves better we can free ourselves from their influence, thus seeing reality for what it really is. Consider this as an invitation for you to do the same as you read this book and as you reflect on your practice.

2

Leadership as Entitlement

In Chapter One I argued that a radical change is needed in the way we think about leadership and in the way we practice leadership. Take the concept of shared leadership, for example. Despite its appeal, this concept may actually be part of the problem. This thought occurred to me when I first encountered the term *distributed leadership*. My first reaction was "old wine in new wineskins." We are pretty good at reinventing old ideas by changing the language of leadership without changing the meaning of leadership. Shared leadership, in this case, was now becoming distributed leadership.

But the more I thought about the concept of distributed leadership the more I realized that not only were we being offered a new meaning for leadership but that we might be on the cusp of a paradigm change, a change in mindscapes. This change could alter not only our understanding of leadership but also our understanding of strategy, change, motivation, collaborative cultures, and a host of other organizational and management concepts.

Sharing leadership, for example, implies that leadership belongs to a designated leader. It is the leader's choice to share or not to share. The dictionary defines *to share* as "to grant or give a share" and *sharing* as "the original holder grants to another the partial use, enjoyment, or possession of a thing." There is wide agreement that effective practice requires principals and other designated leaders to share the leadership responsibilities they have by virtue of their rank or position. But when leadership is said to be owned by one person or group of persons at a given rank and then shared with others who do not own it, the others become dependent. Further, the practice of others is likely to be shaped by designated leaders. The way things work now, designated leaders have a right to decide how much, with whom, and under what circumstances leadership will be shared. But for leadership to be effective it needs to be fully resourced. This happens when one's responsibility and authority are matched. And this happens when others have the necessary discretion to lead. When there is not enough discretion, there will not be enough leadership to get the job done. This is a problem not just for teachers. Principals also are faced with under-resourced leadership sharing from above. Increasingly the responsibilities they have far exceed the authority they have. No matter how hard they try to lead, when their discretion is compromised so is their leadership practice.

Leadership as a Practice

Must leadership always be linked with positions or could we think of it as being a function too? One way to blur the distinction between position and function is to view the principalship, for example, as a practice whose responsibilities, functions, and actions are shared by principals and teachers. Teaching, too, could be thought of as a practice shared by teachers and principals. In each case sharing is a characteristic of the practice itself. It is not a separate decision controlled by a person. Principals, for example, are entitled to assume the role of principal teacher if they have the expertise and commitment to do so. And teachers, too, are entitled to assume leadership roles as long as the roles they assume are matched with their levels of competency and commitment.

Thus an alternative to the way we usually think about shared leadership is to view leadership as an entitlement that is linked to a practice. This leadership isn't indiscriminately distributed but distributed to those who have a legitimate entitlement to claim it. Entitlement is most often legitimized by expertise and commitment. Those who get to lead—indeed those who have a responsibility to lead—are those who have the will, expertness, temperament, and skills to help us achieve our goals in a particular area at a particular time. Others are entitled to step forward as leaders in other areas.

Entitlement is the solution to the ability-authority gap. The principle of ability-authority was proposed by the noted organizational theorist Victor Thompson in 1965. He argued that the major problem facing modern organizations is the growing gap that exists between those who have authority to act but not the ability to lead and those who have the ability to act but not the authority to lead. Entitlement seeks to place those who have the ability to act in the forefront of decision making. In successful schools, organizational structures promote authority based on ability. In schools and school districts where it is necessary for authority to be formally linked to position in the organizational hierarchy, day-by-day practice is characterized by formal and informal delegation of this authority to those with ability and commitment. But the long-term solution is to separate leadership from position by entitling anyone who qualifies to lead. As Martin Sorrell, CEO of the WPP Group in London, phrases it, "The people at the so-called bottom of an organization know more about what is going on than the people at the top. The people in the trenches are in the best position to make critical decisions. It's up to leaders to give these people the freedom and the resources that they need" ("Is Your Company Up to Speed?" 2003, p. 86).

But will changing the conditions for deciding who will lead result in confusion? And will this confusion result in losing control over deciding what needs to be done, how, and by whom? I don't think so. Separating leadership from position does not undermine a teacher's authority, a principal's authority, or a superintendent's authority. Position still counts, as does legal authority. It does mean, however, that in spite of position and legal authority, leadership remains an entitlement. If we do not, for example, have the necessary ability to lead then we do not have the entitlement to lead. Still, we remain in charge. It is still our responsibility, for example, to provide the necessary resources and management supports, to assess how well we are doing, and to otherwise look after the school. An important part of our job, as Bennis and Nanus (1985) remind us, is to provide the management support to ensure that people do things right at the same time we focus leadership on doing right things for teaching and learning. Al West, head of SEI Investments, calls entitlement "fluid leadership." In his words, "People figure out what they're good at, and that shapes what their roles are. There's not just one leader. Different people lead during different parts of the process" (cited in "Is Your Company Up to Speed?", 2003, p. 82).

But, you might argue, by distributing leadership to everyone who is entitled we will create a situation where there are too many coaches and not enough players. The research says otherwise. The work of Arnold Tannenbaum (1968) is a good example. He found that designated leaders can actually increase control by giving up authority. Furthermore, he noted, power and influence should not be considered zero-sum economic concepts. Sharing power means more power for everyone—power has the capacity to expand, and distributing more power within an organization resulted in more power for everyone—including the designated leaders. And more power for everyone seems to be linked to both increased satisfaction and performance.

Tannenbaum found that the total amount of power and influence that existed in an enterprise across ranks was a better predictor of satisfaction and performance than was the relative amount of power and influence held by any one group as compared with another. His ideas apply as well to schools. Imagine, for example, two schools with influence patterns on a 1–10 scale as follows:

	School A	School B
Parents	2	4
Teachers	3	6
Principal	4	9
Sum of power	9	19
Sum of differences	2	5

In School A power is fairly equally distributed among parents, teachers, and principals with a difference of 1 noted for teachers as compared with principals and for parents as compared with teachers. In School B, the differences are 3 and 2, indicating power is distributed in a somewhat "less equal" manner. The sum of power in School A, however, is less than one-half of that for School B (9 versus 19). Tannenbaum would predict that though the distribution within School B is less equal, B would report higher levels of satisfaction and higher levels of performance across the board, the reasoning being that school site B was more empowered than A. School A resembles how many schools share power. Though sharing is equal, it is not very deep, reflecting an arbitrary decision by an authority figure. The amount shared depends on the dispositions of the power holders. In School B, the distribution of power may not be a function of a person but of an organization and the needs that must be met for that organization to be successful.

Liberating Leadership

Viewing leadership as a group activity linked to a practice rather than just an individual activity linked to a person helps match the expertise we have in a school with the problems and situations we face. Of course, both leadership as an individual activity and leadership as a group activity linked to a practice are necessary. But including group activity liberates leadership and provides the framework we need for widespread involvement in improving schools.

If leadership is a practice shared by many, then it must be distributed among those who are in the right place at the right time (situation) and among those who have the unique competence to get the job done correctly (ability). The unique competence requirement determines who, among those with the necessary ability, should step forward to assume responsibility for leadership. This is an important point, for responsibility is the flip side of entitlement. A person who is entitled to lead should be responsible for leading. Someone who refuses this entitlement without good reason thereby refuses responsibility—raising moral questions of fairness, loyalty, and commitment.

Distributed Leadership

Since the leadership functions needed vary with the situation, the abilities needed also vary. These complexities demonstrate just how untenable it is for us to continue to think about leadership as essentially an individual activity. As Spillane, Halverson, and Diamond (2001) see it, "We develop a perspective on leading practice that attends to leaders' thinking and action *in situ*. Leadership involves the identification, acquisition, allocation, coordination, and use of the social, material, and cultural resources necessary to establish the conditions for the possibility of teaching and learning" (p. 24). They further state, "By taking leadership practice in the school as the unit of analysis, rather than an individual leader, our distributed theory of leadership focuses on how leadership practice is distributed among both positional and informal leaders" (p. 24).

Since Spillane and his colleagues ground leadership in the activities that must be assumed if school goals and purposes are to be achieved, then it is the tasks around which leadership as a practice are planned, organized, and evaluated that must be identified and understood. Though visions and other big ideas are essential, they are no more essential than the insides of leadership—the practical goals that must be identified and the practical tasks that must be organized and completed for teaching and learning to take place.

Practical goals and practical tasks are best addressed when roles and functions are brought together.

Certainly there are prerogatives that come from roles and positions. But these prerogatives are subordinate to the functions and activities that must be completed and to the abilities that people bring to their achievement. As Spillane and his colleagues (2001) explain, "The school improvement literature identifies several functions that are thought essential for instructional leadership, including constructing and selling an instructional vision; building norms of trust, collaboration, and academic press; supporting teacher development; and monitoring instruction and innovation" (p. 24). These are the functions that provide the subject matter for setting goals, assigning responsibility, developing plans, and engaging in other activities.

In today's reform climate, supervision with learning in mind is best understood as both a role and a function.[1] When, for example, principals, department chairs, central office subject-matter specialists, and other formally designated supervisors visit classrooms to help teachers improve their practice, they are exercising their formal supervisory roles. They do this by engaging in such functions as observing teaching and providing helpful comments, helping teachers to reflect on their practice, teaching a demonstration lesson, suggesting items teachers might include in their portfolios, disaggregating test score data, and conducting formal evaluations of teaching as required by district or state policy.

But others, too, engage in supervisory functions, even though they are not formal supervisors. Teachers, for example, engage in supervisory functions when they visit each other's classes to learn and to provide help, to share and review each other's planning, to examine together samples of student work, to pore over the most recent test scores together, to puzzle together over whether assignments they are

---

[1] The remainder of this section comes from *Supervision: A Redefinition* (Sergiovanni and Starratt, 2002), pp. 4–5. Used with permission of McGraw-Hill Companies.

giving students are appropriate or whether student performance levels meet important standards, to share portfolios, to work on a common assessment, and to engage in other activities that increase their learning, the learning of their colleagues, and the quality of teaching and learning that students receive.

The supervisory functions are so important in helping schools contribute effectively to rigorous and authentic learning that they cannot be rationed to just those who have formal supervisory responsibilities. Principals and other formal supervisors, therefore, have two broad responsibilities:

- To provide the most effective supervision they can for teachers, *and*

- To provide the conditions, help, and support teachers need to engage in the supervisory functions for themselves as part of their daily routine

By fulfilling these responsibilities, both formal and informal supervisors can build a culture of supervision in the school that includes a commitment to continuous learning. Within this culture teachers become members of communities of practice. Communities of practice are formed as teachers come together in a common effort to help each other teach and learn, to care for each other, and to work together in advancing student academic achievement. The ties that bind teachers and their work together within such communities are such that teachers think of themselves as being less involved in a collection of individual practices and more involved in a single, shared practice of teaching.

Communities of Practice

In many situations, ability authority and position authority will be matched. For example, the principal who knows more about organizing effective writing workshops for students than does the teacher brings both position authority and ability authority to bear in putting together such a workshop. But when we are in a situation where the teacher knows more than the principal, then it is ability authority and not position authority that must be honored. The more likely situation is when both teacher and principal bring substantial amounts of ability authority to their work. The principal may have some special insights about writers' workshops and the teacher may have other insights. That is why thinking about leadership as a practice makes more sense than thinking about leadership as an expression of individual agency. Practices may be singular or group. Regarding leadership as a practice helps us to see teachers and principals as members of communities of practice within which knowledge is used and exchanged to achieve goals with little regard for roles and positions. Within communities of practice, for example, leadership activity takes place at the level of the community rather than at the level of individuals. What is important is the kind of leadership this community needs and whether this community is indeed getting the leadership it needs. The alternative is to assign responsibility to a person before the fact and under the dubious assumption that the person chosen possesses the interests, dispositions, knowledge, and skills to successfully accept that responsibility for all situations, every time.

Reciprocity Is Key

Roles are markers that help define what a person should do, a concept discussed in more detail in Chapter Three. But roles are definers for contracts too. This is especially true when role responsibilities are reciprocal and role relationships are interactive. My role is to fly the airplane and your role is to navigate. We need each other to have a successful trip. And finally, roles are definers for covenants—the most sacred obligations and commitments we have toward each other, toward the school and toward its purposes. Roles as definers of covenants obligate us to meet, even exceed, our responsibilities toward each other and toward the institutions and communities. Roles as markers work in schools when teachers, parents, and students are properly motivated. Roles as contracts work as long as parties to the contract get what they want in exchanges that resemble trades. Roles as covenants work when we feel morally obliged to meet our responsibilities even if we don't want to and whether we are getting something we want in exchange or not.

All these definitions of roles are played out in the everyday lives of schools, and all of these roles contribute to the development of relationships that make schools work. Thus the question is not which role definition is appropriate but what is the proper balance among them. Which definition of roles, for example, belongs at the center and which definition of roles belongs at the periphery in our family lives, in our communal relationships, in schools, and in our social lives? When considering these kinds of organizations and groups, the answer for me is clear: roles defined as covenants should be at the center and roles defined as markers or as contracts should be at the periphery.

Value-Added Leadership

Ideas such as reciprocity and role relationships, and matching entitlements to lead with responsibility and ability, contain powerful moral undercurrents that can be used to bring people together to lead and learn. There are two basic ways to get schools to work well for students. One way involves the use of controls to force everyone to do the right thing. The other way involves the building of commitment to compel everyone to do the right thing. The first way pushes from the outside and the second way pulls from the inside. *Strengthening the Heartbeat* is a book about pulling from the inside—and that way relies on leadership and learning together.

Margaret Szabo and Linda Lambert (2002) propose a theory of action in leadership that includes the following questions:

- *Purposing:* Where are we going?

- *Doing:* How will we get there?

- *Constructing:* What are we working on and learning about?

- *Reframing:* How else might we view this?

- *Transforming:* How far have we gone? And what difference does it make?

Lambert believes that each dimension of this theory of action depends upon the reciprocal processes that define relationships. Leadership, she argues, is beyond the person and beyond any individual role. Leadership is, instead, a pattern of relationships. Thus to her, "Leadership is a reciprocal process that enables participants in an educational community to construct meaning that leads toward a shared purpose of schooling" (2002, p. 42).

Friendship and Distributed Leadership

The importance of relationships in increasing the value of leadership is often underplayed. Yet, as Nora Bredes (cited in Hauser, 2002) points out, leaders usually have a solid though invisible support system that not only helps build their capacities to lead but compounds the effects of their leadership. For women in particular this support system exists in the form of deep friendships. Friendship and the leadership it breeds is not the same as congeniality. Nor is it dominated by the routine exchange of wants and needs. When leadership and friendship are linked there is usually a set of ideas, values, or purposes that knits the two together.

Friendship is a way that leadership can be distributed across individuals who are partners to a relationship. The Susan B. Anthony Center for Women's Leadership at the University of Rochester uses the remarkable friendship between Susan B. Anthony and Elizabeth Cady Stanton to illustrate this point. Though bound to common purposes that bonded them together in a close friendship, Anthony and Cady Stanton brought different gifts to their relationship:

Anthony was described as the "Napoleon" of the suffragist movement. Hers was the organizational and tactical genius. She displayed her skill by appearing before every Congress between 1869 and 1906 on behalf of women's suffrage. Stanton's role was that of thinker and writer. She worked unremittingly for the women's movement in all its phases, including divorce reform, birth control, the challenge to religious assumptions which opposed legal rights for women. At the same time, she managed a household of seven children. Anthony often went to Stanton's home and helped take care of these children in order to free her fellow suffragist for the intellectual work of which the latter was so capable [Susan B. Anthony Center for Women's Leadership, 2002a, p. 2].

And further,

Anthony and Stanton inspired each other to fight for change. They were abolitionists, temperance activists, and, of course, tireless champions for women's rights and suffrage. Unmarried and without children of her own, Anthony became "Aunt Susan" to Stanton's seven boys and girls. She stirred soup pots and cleaned banged knees to give Stanton time to write speeches, petitions and leaflets. When Stanton couldn't leave home to help rally the troops, Anthony went, thinking of her friend and finding extra power in her words [Susan B. Anthony Center for Women's Leadership, 2002b, p. 2]

By distributing leadership across people who are part of a relationship, leadership is strengthened.

Donaldson (2001) argues that good leadership is invitational leadership. It is a leadership that invites others to be the leaders too. Accepting this invitation requires the distribution of roles and responsibilities among many people. A significant aspect of this distribution creates a strong web of relationships that include teachers, parents, and students as well as administrators and include informal leaders as well as formal leaders. It is not just the lead teacher, the student council, the governance committee of the PTA, or the new administrator on the block that is invited to lead. Exercising leadership on behalf of the school and its learning purposes becomes not only common but obligatory. Having an obligation to lead raises the stakes from managerial to moral. In Donaldson's words, "I introduce a model of leadership residing in a collective relationship where participants are both 'shapers of' and 'shaped by' one another" (p. 41). For him the heartbeat of leadership is a relationship, not a person or a process.

Common purpose, commitment, and action in community are the secrets to building communities of responsibility. Central is the presence of an idea structure and the presence of a common set of commitments that bonds people together in a relationship of trust and caring and binds them to important values, purposes, and responsibilities. The genius of communities of responsibility is their ability to generate distributed leadership as the source of authority, not hierarchy or personality. When this goal is achieved a community of responsibility is created. How communities of responsibility work will be the theme of Chapter Three.

3

Making Visions Useful

Successful schools know how to make their visions useful. They do this by turning visions into action statements. These action statements provide pathways for what needs to be done and become standards for evaluating effectiveness. As a result, schools transform from ordinary organizations to communities of responsibility.

Most of us realize that the image of school as community is important and can be used to help make our schools more caring and productive places for both teachers and students. Even more important is to strive to make schools communities of responsibility (see for example, Sergiovanni, 2000, pp. 59–67). This strategy is not only good in itself but is a powerful pathway to school effectiveness. In this chapter community is viewed as a moral enterprise. Communities spring from common understandings that provide members with a sense of identity, belonging, and involvement that results in the creation of tightly held webs of meaningful relationships that have moral overtones. Important is the idea of mosaic. Common understandings are different from scripts. Like mosaics (Etzioni, 1996/1997), which contain many different elements, common understandings are the frame and glue that provide enough coherence in a school to hold everything together.

Communities of responsibility not only fit this description but go beyond by building into their cultures a capacity for self-regulation that ensures both internal and external accountability. Not only do members of the community share enough of a common focus, they also feel obliged to embody this focus in their behavior. Communities of responsibility are not easy to cultivate in schools. Once established, however, they become powerful substitutes for the bureaucratic and personality-based leadership that now seems to dominate schools. Within communities leadership is defined by its source of authority—an authority that is embedded in ideas that connect us and encourage us to respond from within. Instead of following *someone*, the emphasis is on following commitments, promises, obligations, validated research, sound principles, agreed-upon standards, and other ideas.

Here are six reasons why community is important in schools:

- Community helps satisfy the need that teachers, students, and parents have to be connected to each other and to the school.

- Community helps everyone in the school to focus on the common good.

- Community provides students with a safe harbor in a stormy sea—a place where they are accepted unconditionally.

- Community supports learning.

- Community builds relationships and responsibility.

- Community connects people to their work for moral reasons that obligate them to respond.

When accompanied by a strong commitment to learning and by steps that clearly demonstrate this commitment to students, being responsive to community leads to improved student performance. Further, providing for the connection needs of teachers, parents, and students and focusing on the common good lead to improved student behavior, stronger bonds of collegiality among the faculty, and more productive relationships with parents (see, for example, Sebring and Bryk, 1996).

Community is something most of us want as it helps us experience the sense and meaning that we need in our lives. Being connected to others and being connected to institutions we value is a way to be connected to ourselves, to know that we belong, to know that we count for something important, to know that we are valued. It is the sense and meaning that teachers get from connections that help to create "collaborative cultures" in schools—a theme of Chapter Six. It is the sense and meaning that students get from connections that hold together student learning communities in schools.

In Chapter One I noted that the link between *communis* and *communitas*—what we hold in common and the moral quality of our relationships with others—is the heart and soul of community. When teachers, for example, come together to share goals and to make a collective commitment to pursue these goals in a certain way, they are creating communities of responsibility. As members of these communities, they promise each other, the students they teach, their principals and other administrators, and the parents of the children they teach to meet certain obligations, and they feel morally obliged to follow through on these promises. When administrators, students, and parents do likewise, they too are creating communities of responsibility. Communities of responsibility are held together by webs of promises and obligations.

Making Visions Useful

Many schools embrace the idea of building networks of communities of responsibility but fail to create them because they don't understand fully how visions work. Vision statements have value. But too often they remain idealized statements that only remotely resemble what is going on in the school. When this happens vision statements are not working documents. They are not used to help make decisions or to assess the decisions that are made. Too many students, teachers, and administrators alike would have to look up their vision if they were asked to describe it. One reason that many vision statements are lots of show and not much tell is that, alone, they fail to provide the direction and fail to spell out the commitments that are needed from various constituent groups to make these visions work. They do not tell us what we need to do and they do not tell us what our responsibilities are for implementing the vision. For this reason we need to move

- From vision and goals to goals and roles

- From goals and roles to obligations and strategies

- From obligations and strategies to actions and pathways

"To answer questions about goals," Joyce Epstein (2001) reminds us, "we must ask questions about roles." She asks:

> Whose dreams are these? Children will like school; work hard; do the best they can; graduate from high school; continue their education; gain employment; and become good citizens, friends, and members of their families. Countless surveys and projects with thousands of educators, families, and students reveal that these are common goals and dreams. Too often, though, these ideals are unattained by this nation's children. How can more students be helped to meet these goals? To answer questions about goals, we must ask questions about roles: What should families do, what should schools and communities do, and what should students do to reach their common objectives for children's futures? [p. 3].

If we refuse to answer questions about roles and refuse to translate roles into obligations and actions, our visions will likely fizzle away.

Richard DuFour, a long-time principal and superintendent in the Adlai Stevenson High School District 125 in Lincolnshire, Illinois, puts it this way: "The challenge is to make the vision come to life, and that challenge can only be met when the various components of the organization make a collective commitment to act in accordance with the vision."[1]

When all we have are lofty vision statements, role relationships are likely to be vague. The nature of their reciprocity is not spelled out and this limits their usefulness. Value is added when visions are accompanied by the promises and commitments each constituent group makes to help move the school closer to its vision. Effective visions obligate people who share them. This obligation ups the ante from visions as management tools to visions as moral statements. Adding role-based reciprocal commitments to vision is an example of practicing value-added leadership. Stevenson High School's vision and the collective commitments needed from constituent groups for this vision to be embodied in practice go hand in hand. Because of the array of collective commitments, Stevenson's vision runs deep and is useful in helping its people make decisions and assess progress. Visions and commitments together obligate people to each other and to their work.

The collective commitments from Stevenson's administrative team, faculty, support staff, students, and parents appear in Exhibit 3.1. As DuFour explains: "The board has created separate task forces for each constituent group to consider the question, 'What

---

[1] References to Richard DuFour and to the collective commitments of various Stevenson constituents are from Stevenson High School (2003), used with permission. DuFour's insights both in this chapter and in Chapter Six have been invaluable and are appreciated. Special thanks also to Dan Galloway, current principal of Stevenson High School, for helping me learn about how and why Stevenson High School works as well as it does.

commitments must our group make and fulfill in order to help move the school closer to what is described in the vision statement?'" These statements of commitment are prefaced by the following directions:

> Please carefully review these statements and then use them in the following two ways:
>
> 1. Use the statement for each group as criteria by which you judge its performance. If you feel we are failing to live up to the commitments we have articulated, bring it to our attention.
> 2. Use the commitment statement for your group as a guideline for your own contribution to helping Stevenson become a better school.

The commitment of each of the constituent groups represents promises, and public promises at that. Teachers, for example, are telling students, administrators, and everyone else what they intend to do to implement the school's vision. Since promises made must be promises kept, Stevenson is not only developing an accountability system that is public but a covenant of obligations that unites its various groups as a community of responsibility.

How Roles, Role Relationships, and Role Sets Work

A covenant of obligations raises the stakes from management commitment to moral commitment. When a moral threshold is reached, teachers, parents, students, and administrators accept their roles and the elements that define them. Roles come with expectations that serve as a compass pointing the way and a beacon lighting the way. Role expectations are not only received but also sent. Expectations sent typically deal with rights, and expectations received typically deal with obligations.

Exhibit 3.1. Stevenson High School Collective Commitments

Stevenson High School Leadership Team Collective Commitments
We will model and promote the behaviors called for in the Stevenson Vision Statement among all members of the Stevenson community. These behaviors include, but are not limited to, open and effective communication, collaborative problem solving and decision making, and high expectations for achievement. They also include consideration and caring for all members of the Stevenson family, a commitment to life-long learning and continuous improvement, and a work ethic that reflects the importance of our mission.

We will recruit and retain individuals who are best suited to advance the vision and goals of the District, and we will create conditions which support their ongoing professional growth.

We will facilitate the development of curricular and co-curricular programs which result in high levels of student engagement, reflect student needs and interests, integrate technology when appropriate for achieving program goals, and enable students to understand and appreciate diverse cultures.

We will develop and implement policies, programs, and procedures to monitor and support collective achievement and individual student success.

We will develop and implement policies, programs, and procedures which result in students assuming increasing responsibilities for their learning, decisions, and actions.

We will recognize and celebrate the efforts and achievements of the members of the Stevenson family.

We will fulfill our responsibilities for good stewardship by managing the District's resources in a manner that addresses the needs of the community, builds community support, and establishes community partnerships.

Stevenson High School Faculty Collective Commitments
We have established these guiding principles as a reflection of our values as teachers and professionals at Stevenson High School. They are intended as a means for informal personal assessment and are not intended to be used in the formal evaluation process. They represent our shared purpose and will continue to guide us as educators.

Exhibit 3.1. Stevenson High School Collective Commitments (*continued*)

1. We will develop curriculum and instructional strategies that promote active involvement for students, provide for their varied experiences and individual abilities, and utilize technology and other tools where appropriate.

2. We will help each student's transition through high school by providing appropriate instruction, monitoring his/her progress, and offering guidance and support services tailored to individual needs.

3. We will model the importance of life-long learning through our ongoing personal and professional development.

4. We will collaborate with one another to create conditions that promote student success and a rewarding professional experience.

5. We will act in a professional manner with integrity and honesty and will develop relationships characterized by caring and respect.

6. We will provide a supportive school atmosphere where everyone feels emotionally, physically, and intellectually safe.

7. We will hold high expectations for student achievement and character, and will encourage students to take responsibility for their lives and the learning process.

8. We will care for our physical environment and school property and will require the same of students.

9. We will communicate with parents about their student's progress in school and will encourage parents to be involved in their children's education.

Stevenson High School Support Staff Collective Commitments

Although we have diverse responsibilities as members of the support staff, each of us is in a position to help Stevenson achieve its mission of success for every student. Furthermore, in fulfilling our respective responsibilities, we share common commitments. These include the following:

1. We will support the collective effort to create the school described in Stevenson's Vision Statement.

2. We will continue to develop and support positive relationships with our colleagues, our students, and our community.

3. We will approach every situation with an open mind and a commitment to continuous improvement.

4. We will participate in effective communication throughout the school and community.

Exhibit 3.1. Stevenson High School Collective Commitments (*continued*)

5. We will promote a safe and nurturing environment that is conducive to the academic and social growth of each individual student.
6. We will model:
   - a commitment to life-long learning
   - appreciation for cultural diversity
   - pride and ownership in the school.

Collective Commitments for Stevenson Students
(adopted by Student Leaders Advisory Council, 1997)
For over thirty years, Stevenson High School has been building a tradition of excellence. As a student of Stevenson, you are asked to help contribute to that tradition. By maintaining high personal expectations for success, utilizing open communication with staff and fellow students, and following the guidelines listed below, you both increase your opportunities for success and help make Stevenson an excellent school.

1. Accept responsibility for your education, decisions, and actions.
2. Act in a way that best represents your school, parents, community, and self to promote a safe, healthy environment in which to learn.
3. Be active in the school and community.
4. Maintain a balance between academics, co-curricular activities, and community projects, continually giving your best effort to each.
5. Support your fellow students and their activities.
6. Respect cultural diversity, individuality, and the choices and rights of others.

Collective Commitments for Stevenson Parents
We, as parents, must first become familiar with the established vision statement of Stevenson High School. We can contribute to the pursuit of that vision and the success of our children when we:

1. Become informed and knowledgeable about the curricular, co-curricular, and student support programs available to students by:
   - carefully reviewing school publications such as the *Curriculum Coursebook*, *Co-Curricular Handbook*, and *Student Guidebook*.
   - attending and participating in parent information programs sponsored by the school.
   - reading *The Minuteman* each month.

Exhibit 3.1. Stevenson High School Collective Commitments (*continued*)

2. Assist our children in making important educational decisions by:
   - helping our children set educational goals which are appropriate to their individual capabilities, interests, and needs.
   - participating in the course selection process.
   - encouraging involvement in school activities.
   - helping our children identify and pursue post-secondary education and career goals.

3. Engage in open and timely communication with the school by:
   - responding to the school's feedback about our children's academic progress and behavior.
   - advising school personnel of any special circumstances or needs of our children.
   - being proactive in asking questions, expressing concerns, and seeking information.

4. Become actively involved in the life of the school by:
   - attending school programs.
   - participating in parent support groups such as the Patriot Parent Association, Booster Clubs, Task Forces, etc.
   - volunteering in the school.
   - acting as an advocate for quality education within the community.
   - utilizing the resources of the school through adult education and community access programs.

5. Help our children become responsible, self-reliant members of the school community by:
   - teaching them to accept responsibility for their own learning, decisions, and behavior.
   - insisting they observe the rules of the school.
   - demonstrating respect, consideration, and cooperation in dealing with others and expecting our children to do the same.

6. Create a supportive environment for learning in our homes by:
   - modeling the importance of life-long learning.
   - providing a quiet time and place for study.
   - helping our students make connections between their learning experiences and their everyday lives.
   - expecting achievement and offering encouragement and praise.

Exhibit 3.1. Stevenson High School Collective Commitments (*continued*)

7. Promote healthy lifestyles by:
   - modeling and supporting responsible lifestyle choices.
   - monitoring the activities of our children and responding to behavior which jeopardizes their health and well-being.
   - becoming informed of the risks associated with teenage use of alcohol, tobacco, and other drugs.
   - discussing and developing family rules which prohibit illegal use of alcohol, tobacco, and other drugs.

The role of student, for example, includes such obligations as to do one's best, to get work in on time, to help other students, and to be respectful. It includes certain rights too. Students have a right to have qualified, competent, and caring teachers, responsive instruction, and a safe environment; to be treated with respect; and to have a voice in what is going on. Leadership is an earned entitlement for students too. Students often know the student subculture best. And students are in the best position to help develop norm systems and ways of doing things or to transform existing norm systems so that they are friendly to the teaching, learning, and caring purposes of the school.

The collective commitment of students to a school vision can be written for them or by them. When it is written by them, students earn still more entitlement to lead. Some administrators and teachers may wonder about whether they want to risk inviting students to spell out the collective commitments that they are prepared to make to help the school achieve its vision. But since the commitments of students and teachers are reciprocal, students are tied to those commitments made by their teachers. Thus these role relationships contain rights and obligations that define the ties that link the roles of teachers and students together. While Stevenson has collective commitments from a variety of constituent groups, it also has a single set of commitments that are owned by everyone who is involved in a common role set.

Similarly, teachers have roles that include rights and responsibilities—as do parents, principals, and others. Sociologists Jerald Hage and Charles Powers (1992) view a *role* as "a package of broadly recognized rights and obligations that define what would be expected of anyone occupying a given position embedded within a system of social relations" (p. 7). Since the heart of any role is rights and responsibilities, roles cannot meaningfully exist without being linked to other roles. The rights and responsibilities of teachers, for example, are understood within the context of rights and responsibilities of students, principals, and parents.

As Hage and Powers explain, "A *role relationship* refers to those rights and obligations commonly taken to define the nature of the tie that links two roles together" (1992, p. 7). Bundles of role relationships result in *role sets*. If these role sets evolve into friendly networks, then even the most difficult of schools will have the moral network to be able to succeed. Networks are *friendly* when role sets are linked to common purposes and shared frameworks for working together. This linkage can transform networks of teachers and networks of students into communities of practice and communities of learners.

When transformed, work roles are joined into a shared practice and that practice introduces moral ties that bond people together and bind them to purposes and obligations. Stevenson, for example, is also known for its "collaborative cultures"—departments or teams of teachers who live, work, and learn together by accepting collective responsibility for curriculum goals, lesson and unit planning and sharing, and the evaluation of student work, the setting of standards, and the development of common assessments. The relationship structure of Stevenson's faculty is made up of role sets, dozens of them, with each being a community of practice committed to leadership and learning together. In Chapter Six I will go into further detail on how collaborative cultures at Stevenson work and the role that the bubbling up of communities of practice plays.

Role: A package of broadly defined rights and obligations.

Role relationships: Rights and responsibilities that link roles together.

Role sets: Bundles of role relationships that, when linked to common purposes, evolve into friendly networks or communities of practice.

Work roles: Patterns of activity and behavior that define how work will be done.

Work roles are patterns of activities and behaviors that emerge from the social context of roles, role relationships, and role sets. These patterns shape how work will be done. As the social context for schools changes from simple to complex, patterns of activities and behaviors change in fundamental ways. Learning becomes even more important. Working together becomes even more important. And leadership distributed across all roles becomes even more important. In today's learning organization work roles are defined "in terms of information gathering, problem solving, the production of creative ideas, and the ability to respond flexibly to new situations or adjust flexibly when interacting with others" (Hage and Powers, 1992, p. 11).

Leading and learning together are important because today's roles make challenging demands on everyone. Typically, today's roles require more mental activity, more information, and more problem solving than those of earlier generations did. These more challenging definitions of duties and obligations mean that more learning is required from everyone. Roles, say Hage and Powers, are "defined by goals for which no certain procedure can be specified, consequently involving a relatively wide range of nonroutine tasks" (p. 13). As a result it is difficult to chart exactly when a particular role activity might be appropriate. Teachers and principals must determine how work will be done and how time will be spent while actually doing their jobs, in effect creating their practice in use. And increasingly, the standard for effective job performance is less and less a sense of completion and more and more a sense of mastery. Quality schooling isn't about seat time, accumulating Carnegie units, and completing other requirements as much as it is about the mastery of standards and other outcomes. As summarized in the box "Leading and Learning Together," complex purposes, interdependent relationships, and the need to create our practice in use require that leadership and learning together become part of any strategy to improve schools.

Leading and Learning Together

• The purposes of schools, the nature of teaching, and the expectations for success are becoming increasingly complex. *As a result, continuous learning is more important.*

• As complexity increases, people become more interdependent, look to each other for support, and are required to pool their intellectual capital to be successful. *As a result, learning together and working together is more important.*

• Complex purposes and complex settings require that problems be solved and decisions be made by those closest to teaching and learning as they create their practice in use. *As a result, leadership distributed throughout the school and school district is more important.*

Relational Trust

In role sets no single person has the power to make things work. Thus members of an effective role set are naturally interdependent and held together by relational trust. Trust is the tie that binds roles together, allowing the creation of role sets that embody reciprocal obligations.

Social capital and community are close cousins of relational trust. They are so close that it is doubtful we would find a school with only one of the cousins. Social capital has to do with the supports that students and teachers need to be effective learners and doers. Relational trust refers to the quality and kind of social exchanges one finds in sets of role relationships. Trust is high when every party to the role set feels supported and safe. Support and safety are provided by social exchanges. Both social capital and relational trust are the DNA of community. They are so integral to both the *communis* and *communitas* aspects of community life that operational definitions of community routinely include them.

Anthony Bryk and Barbara Schneider (2002), who coined the term for use in education, describe *relational trust* as follows:

> Relational trust views the social exchanges of schooling as organized around a distinct set of role relationships: teachers with students, teachers with other teachers, teachers with parents and with their school principal. Each party in a role relationship maintains an understanding of his or her role obligations and holds some expectations about the role obligations of the other. [They see relational trust as] a complex web of social exchanges [that] conditions the basic operations of schools. Embedded in the daily social routines of schools is an interrelated set of mutual dependencies among all key actors: students, teachers, principals and administrators, and parents. These structural dependencies create feelings of vulnerability for the individuals involved [p. 20].

Relational trust, in other words, is the antidote to the vulnerability that we are likely to experience in our lives as members of role sets in schools. For example, no matter how deep and thorough are the exchanges among Stevenson High School's teachers, students, parents, and administrators, without trusting relationships these exchanges would likely encourage self-protection and holding back, severely limiting the capacity for collaboration, learning, and improved performance.

As a result of their extensive research on school improvement in Chicago and in other places, Bryk and Schneider (2002) found the following in the elementary schools they studied:

- First, collective decision making with broad teacher buy-in occurs more readily in schools with strong relational trust (p. 122).

- Second, when relational trust is strong, reform initiatives are more likely to be deeply engaged by school participants and to diffuse broadly across the organization (p. 122).

- Third, relational trust foments a moral imperative to take on the hard work of school improvement (p. 123).

In sum, Bryk and Schneider found that relational trust was an important catalyst for the development of a supportive work culture characterized by school commitment and a positive orientation toward change. And relational trust was an important catalyst for the development of a facilitative work structure that included the development of professional community for making decisions together and for supporting teacher learning. Supportive work cultures and facilitative work structures, they found, result in higher levels of student engagement and improvements in student learning (p. 124).

What About Students?

In my experience schools rarely take the opportunity to routinely seek and use student ideas. They seem particularly shy in involving students in matters of academic policy and discipline policy. You can find out if I am off the mark by asking five administrators, ten teachers, and fifteen students to respond to the following two questions:[2]

1. How often does your school ask for and use the ideas of students about academic matters (for example, course content, teacher plans, methods of teaching, setting standards, evaluation)?

2. How often does your school work for and use the ideas of students about nonacademic matters (for example, discipline policy, learning about and changing norms of the student subculture, rules of conduct)?

Use a 4-point scale as follows to record your responses:

Rarely	Sometimes	Often	Very Often
1	2	3	4

It is a given that teachers and other adults in schools are more likely to accept and be committed to things they have a hand in creating or deciding. Why would this not be the case for students as well? If we are not seeking and using students' ideas often, we are squandering an important resource for making schools better both academically and socially. But there are fears. Can students be trusted? What would we do with ideas we can't possibly use? Will students be responsible enough to be involved in matters that are central to what we do in schools? Some will respond, "No thanks! They can vote on whether we will sign a contract with Coke or

[2] These questions are adapted from "The Profile of a School," a seventy-two-item school climate inventory developed by Rensis Likert Associates of Ann Arbor, Michigan, in 1977.

Pepsi, and they can advise us on the style of the new basketball uniforms. That is as far as we will go." But we have nothing to fear and everything to gain if we get teacher-student role sets right.

The Teacher-Student Role Set

In the best of worlds teachers and students are bonded together in a common commitment that requires the acceptance of responsibility by each for meeting their reciprocal role obligations. Just as it is important that teachers try their best, so it is important that students, too, try their best. Just as it is important for teachers to help students be successful, so it is important that students help teachers be successful. Bonds of obligations are the missing ingredient in too many schools, and despite good wishes and valiant efforts this void makes teaching and learning an upstream swim. But it need not be that way. Schools can help teaching and learning become a downstream swim by committing themselves to becoming communities of responsibility.

In a U.K. study John MacBeath (1999) asked a group of Year 8 girls to think about and then describe a good teacher that they had. Here is the list they created, with MacBeath's comments:

> The good teacher
>
> | | |
> |---|---|
> | is kind | is forgiving |
> | is generous | tells the truth |
> | listens to you | makes allowances |
> | encourages you | stands up for you |
> | has faith in you | treats people equally |
> | keeps confidences | makes you feel clever |
> | likes teaching children | cares for your opinion |
> | likes teaching their subject | doesn't give up on you |
> | helps you like their subject | helps people who are slow |

takes time to explain things   makes sure you understand

helps you when you're stuck   allows you to have your say

tells you how you are doing

One teacher suggested the list should be put up on the classroom wall as a reference point for both the teacher and her students. Another agreed to do this once they had gone through a similar exercise for the good student. With two such lists side by side on the classroom wall it was much easier for the teacher to hold her students to account as well as being reminded by them when she was not meeting expectations. Good teachers and good students do not exist in some kind of idealised vacuum. They are a product of one another's expectations and behaviour. In the language of biology their relationship is "symbiotic" [1999, p. 60].

Can younger students participate in conversations about reciprocal role expectations and about their teacher-student role set? MacBeath (1999) responds yes, sharing the following list created by Year 2/3 students:

The good teacher

is very clever	has got courage
doesn't shout	helps you with spelling
helps you every day	helps you to read
is not bossy	marks your work
has faith in you	helps you with mistakes
is funny	tells you clearly what to do
is patient	is good at work [pp. 61–62]

The sharing of expectations and making these expectations explicit only works when role sets such as parent and teacher,

teacher and administrator, and student and teacher respond, and when their responses are reciprocal, and the interactions of participants are characterized by trust. There is a message here for those who seek to lead. The virtues of serving, caring, respecting, empowering, and helping without asking for anything in return are far more powerful motivational devices than is the art for manipulation of motivational science that seeks to trade need fulfillment for compliance. The altruistic love and the sense of duty modeled in those virtues builds the kind of *communis* and *communitas* that not only bonds teachers together (and members of other role sets together) as colleagues and fellows but binds them to obligations and commitments as well. This binding compels them to rise to the occasion and to do their best. When we get community right, we learn how to turn visions into collective commitments and collective commitments into actions that make the school a better place for teachers and students alike. This coming together to share moral commitments is the power of creating communities of responsibility. This is the power of *ubunta*, a word South African educator Susan Lynham (Personal communication, May 28, 2003) draws from the Xhosa tribe of southern Africa. She suggests that the Xhosa have captured the essence of community with *ubunta*, which means: "I am because *you* are, and *you* are because *we* are."

4

Hope, Trust, Community,
and Other Virtues

Schools teach their culture best when they embody purposes, values, norms, and obligations in their everyday activities. Although this principle is widely accepted in word, it is often neglected in deed. The heartbeat of leadership and the heartbeat of schools are strengthened when word and deed are one. And this happens when leadership and virtue work together. Clarence Walton's words are helpful here:

> The question is not whether virtue can be taught but how it may be taught. Example, not exhortation, and practice, not principle, take priority: carpenters become carpenters by building houses; pianists become pianists by playing the piano; managers become leaders by leading. The same is true of character: people become virtuous by practicing virtue and by living with moral mentors. If, for any reason, an organization becomes sidetracked, only managers of sound character can restore a sense of direction. Disciplined organizations reflect disciplined leaders whose honed abilities lead them to behave consistently, almost instinctively, in moral ways [1988, pp. 177–178].

The philosopher Robert K. Fullinwider believes that schools and other agents of society need to teach and live four groups of virtues: moral, intellectual, communal, and political. Our responsibility as leaders is to provide the moral environment of support for the virtues and to model them. These are the virtues that Fullinwider (cited in Walton, 1988, p. 169) recommends:

Moral	Intellectual	Communal	Political
Honesty	Thoughtfulness	Neighborliness	Commitment to the Common Good
Truthfulness	Strength of Mind	Charity	Respect for the Law
Decency	Curiosity	Self-Support	Responsible Participation
Courage			Helpfulness
Justice			Cooperativeness
			Respect for Others

Lee Bolman and Terry Deal (1995) have pointed out that there are many pathways to effective leadership. But, they add, when we look deeper, qualities that are consistent across most effective leaders emerge. Among them are focus, passion, wisdom, courage, and integrity. Effective leaders know what is important and focus on it, care deeply about their work, have learned from both their successes and failures, take calculated risks, and are people you can trust. It is clear from Bolman and Deal's work and from Fullinwider's work that virtues are at the center of what leadership is and how it works.

In this chapter I explore four powerful virtues: hopefulness, trust, piety, and civility. These virtues were chosen because of the roles they can play in transforming school cultures. In these transformed schools students experience academic success as they experience a caring environment. This is not to suggest that the other virtues Fullinwider mentions are unimportant. They are indeed important. But they are insufficient to bring about the kind of success needed in today's schools. Peter Senge (1990, echoing Archimedes) puts it this way: "Give me a lever long enough. . . . and single-handed I can move the world" (p. 3). Adding hopefulness, trust, piety, and civility to the others places the four at the core of our leadership practice and gives us the leverage we need for improving even the most challenging schools.

The Virtue of Hope

Perhaps the most important and perhaps the most neglected leadership virtue is hope. One reason why hope is neglected is because of management theories that tell us to look at the evidence, to be tough as nails, to be objective, and in other ways to blindly face reality. But facing reality rather than relying on hope means accepting reality as it is. Relying on hope rather than facing reality means working to change reality—hopefully. Leaders can be both hopeful and realistic as long as the possibilities for change remain open. Being realistic differs from facing reality in important ways. Being realistic means calculating the odds with an eye to optimism, aware of the consequences of fate without being resigned to the inevitability of a situation or circumstance.

Why should leaders be hopeful? Because the evidence suggests hope can change events for the better. It is widely accepted that sick people who are hopeful members of support groups that provide encouragement, prayer, or other forms of targeted social capital get healthier and stay healthier than do sick people who do not have the benefit of this hopeful social capital. In her review of the literature on hope and health, for example, Sharon Roset finds compelling evidence to link the two. In her words, "Findings in the health sciences show a positive relationship between biochemical reactions, attributed to hopefulness, and its effect upon illness. Oncologist Carl Simonton has found that when cancer patients respond to the challenges before them with 'feelings of hope and anticipation, the organism translates them into biological processes that begin to restore balance and to revitalize the immune system' (quoted in Carter, 1996, p. 1). Medical researchers find that a sense of hopefulness, from an increased sense of control, is connected with biological changes that enhance physical, as well as mental, health" (Roset, 1999, p. 7).

Hope and Wishing

Hope is often confused with wishing. But hope is grounded in reality, not wishful thinking. It is, to use Menninger, Mayman, and Pruyser's term, "realistic hope." They say, "Realistic hope. . . . is based on the attempt to understand the concrete conditions of reality, to see one's own role in it realistically, and to engage in such efforts of thoughtful action as might be expected to bring about the hoped-for change. The affect of hope, in this case, has an activating effect. It helps in the mobilization of the energies needed for activity" (Menninger, Mayman, and Pruyser, 1963, pp. 385–386, as quoted in Roset, 1999, p. 41).

The activating effect of hope makes the difference, not only for motor activity but also for the activity of thought or of relating to other people. Wishful leaders are just that—wishful. They take no deliberate action to make their wishes come true. Hopeful leaders, on the other hand, react actively to what they hope for and deliberately strive to turn hopefulness into reality. Here are the contrasts:

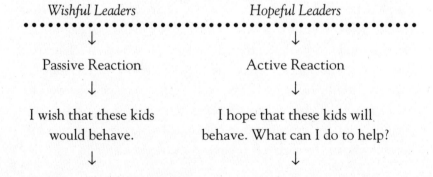

Wishful Leaders	*Hopeful Leaders*
↓	↓
Passive Reaction	Active Reaction
↓	↓
I wish that these kids would behave.	I hope that these kids will behave. What can I do to help?
↓	↓

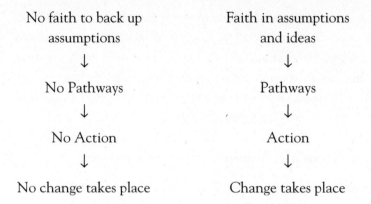

Consider, for example, a couple having financial problems. The bank was threatening to repossess their home and cars. Credit cards were no longer being accepted. Seeing no other way out they hoped (or did they wish?) that they would win the lottery. They prayed hard to God for just that reason. A voice from above said to them, "Yes. Yes, you will win the lottery." After nothing happened during the following week, the couple prayed again as hard as they could. And again the voice spoke, "You will win the lottery." Still another week of praying and still no lottery win. Finally in desperation they said to God, "Look, you promised us. You owe us!" Again the voice came from above: "You will win the lottery, but you have to buy a ticket first."

Faith

Hope and faith go together. Faith comes from commitment to a cause, from strong beliefs in a set of ideas, and from other convictions. "Hope is so closely linked to faith that the two tend to blend into one. The Bible says that 'faith is the substance of things hoped for' (Hebrews 11:1). This is true of faith in God, but it is also true of all other faith. No matter what we put our faith *in*, when faith goes, hope goes with it. In some ways, hope *is* faith—faith with our eyes on possibilities for the future" (Smedes, 1998, p. 21, as quoted in Roset, 1999, p. 48).

This discussion is now getting closer to how hope works to help schools become more effective. Faith is often communicated as a set of assumptions that are assumed to be true. And being true, we can be hopeful that once announced to the world they will come alive, they will be accepted, and they will stir others to action. We might have faith, for example, that

- All children can learn given the right conditions.

- Students can take responsibility for their own learning if we get the student-teacher role set and other important role sets right.

- Schools can become transformed into caring learning communities.

- Teachers want to be self-managing and under the right conditions will take responsibility for their own learning.

- Given the opportunity and the training even the poorest of parents can be effective partners in the education of their children.

- If we provide enough support to students all will succeed.

- Every teacher can be a leader if the circumstances are right and if the issues seem important enough.

These assumptions are not just articles of faith. They suggest pathways that bring faith and action together. We can hope, for example, that students will succeed, but we need to provide the necessary support if we wish to avoid wishful thinking.

Leaders have an important responsibility here. If their own hopefulness is based on faith in a set of assumptions, and if these assumptions come to be shared by others in their school community, then a powerful force of ideas will have been created. These ideas provide the basis for a school to become a community of hope, and these ideas can fuel the school's efforts to turn this hope into reality. Developing a community of hope elevates the work of leadership to the level of moral action. Leadership as moral action is a struggle to do the right thing according to some sense of values, according to some sense of what it means to be a human being. Leaders need to be concerned with what is good as well as what is effective. It is in what is good that we find faith and it is in what is good that this faith becomes the basis for our hopefulness.

From Hope to Action

Action was the key differentiator in the comparison of hopeful leaders and wishful leaders. Hope is based on articles of faith that function as assumptions. These assumptions provide the impetus for doing things that will change hopes into realities. "Hope is a valuable asset for children, adolescents and adults. As conceptualized by Snyder, Harris, and others (1991), hope is a cognitive set comprised of goals, pathways, and agency. Individuals with high hope possess goals, find pathways to these goals, navigate around obstacles, and develop agency to reach their goals" (McDermott, Pedrotti, Edwards, and Houske, 2002, pp. 274–275).

Realizing our hopes in a deliberate way requires that they be transformed into goals—goals that lend themselves to the development of practical pathways. Having the will and determination to travel these pathways, no matter what the obstacles encountered, is the windup key. Unless this key is turned there will be no action. And what first appears as hope winds up being wishful thinking.

We might think of deliberate efforts to turn hope into reality as a process that requires answering the following questions:

- *What are our goals?* Goals are what we hope for.

- *What are our pathways?* Pathways are the routes we decide to take to realize our hopes.

- *What are the obstacles we face?* Obstacles are the barriers that we must overcome.

- *How committed are we to agency, to actually doing something to realize our hopes?* Agency is our determined and persistent effort to travel the pathways.

- *Is efficacy present in sufficient strength?* Efficacy gauges the extent to which we believe we can make a difference and that our efforts will be successful.

- *If efficacy is low, how can it be strengthened?*

The question of efficacy is critical. Do we believe we are able to learn what we must and to use what we learn to be successful in realizing our hopes? The jury is still out on which view of human nature will prevail—optimistic or pessimistic. But I believe that hopeful leaders recognize potentials in persons and in situations. They believe that "what people can achieve, or aspire to, is just as surely part of human nature, just as surely summoned by the human condition, as are more negative traits and dimensions" (Selznick, 2002, p. 70).

Faith, as Wilkins (1989) says, is linked to motivation—and this is good news. Teachers and students decide to stay with a school and to do their best based on faith. Wilkins points out, "If they have faith in the fairness and the ability of the organization [organizational efficacy] and in their own ability to make valued contributions [individual efficacy], then they are likely to be motivated to work for the good of the organization" (p. 27). He notes further, "When people feel that they have the opportunity to grow, to make mistakes and learn from them. . . . they can eventually make valued contributions, they are more likely to continue to be motivated even when they fail occasionally" (p. 29). Wishful thinking is avoided, then, by deliberately taking action and deliberately providing the context for both organizational and individual efficacy. There is, in a sense, a kind of psychological magic that helps us to move from hope to action, and there are also deliberate pathways that we can travel to make this transformation.

Gompers Elementary: A School of Hope

The Gompers Elementary School in Detroit is an example of how faith fuels hope and how hope encourages the heartbeat of a school. In this case it was faith in the Comer process, officially known as the School Development Program (SDP), that made the difference. The Comer process is based on the philosophy and work of James Comer and his colleagues at Yale University's Child Study Center. The nine components of the process provided the structure and means for answering the key questions outlined in the preceding section, thereby helping Gompers turn hope into reality. Asking, What are our purposes? and What are the obstacles we must overcome to realize our purposes? proved particularly important. These are the nine components of the Comer process, summarized from his 1980 book (pp. 281–285):

- School planning and management team

- Parents' program

- Mental health team

- Comprehensive school plan

- Staff development needed to implement plan

- Periodic assessment and modification of plan

- No-fault policy; focus on problem solving

- Consensus decision making

- Collaboration; leading and learning together

Hope Based on Faith

The Samuel Gompers Elementary School houses about 350 students in an economically distressed neighborhood in the city of Detroit.[1] Ninety-three percent of the students are African American. Based on Free and Reduced Lunch applications, 93 percent of the students live at the poverty level. "Our children come to us with basic needs for food, clothing, safe shelter, and security. Many of our students have never seen a dentist, and many have not been immunized prior to the start of school. *Based on the indicators of children at-risk, such as poverty, transience, and single parent homes, 96% of our students are technically at-risk.* Before we can assess the educational needs of the children, basic needs must first be met" (Samuel Gompers Elementary School, 2000, p. 10).

The Comer process is hopeful because it "rejects the notion that low-income parents cannot adequately prepare children for school and that the children cannot perform school tasks at a reasonable level" (Comer, 1980, p. 38). Further, the Comer process rejects any suggestion that teachers, principals, and other school people are not willing and able to develop the necessary approaches, interests, and skills needed for kids to succeed academically, socially, psychologically, and morally. In fact one of the articles of faith of the Comer process is that academic progress cannot be made unless other needs are taken care of. In Comer's words, "Most programs designed to improve schooling fail because they do not adequately address the developmental needs of children and the potential for conflict in the relationship between home and school, among school staff, and among staff and students" (p. 38). Provide for student needs and

---

[1] The Gompers story is drawn from the school's 2000 Blue Ribbon Application. The principal at the time was Marilee Bylsma. Other Gompers faculty members who played key roles in preparing the Blue Ribbon Application were Nekeya Irby, Barb Krupiel, July Pita, Glenn Ellen Rubright, and Joan Sheehan. At this writing Gale Lewis is the principal of Gompers.

provide a supportive climate and you provide the conditions for academic learning.

Having faith in the assumptions underlying the Comer process puts Gompers in a good position to succeed. Gompers, for example, questions the generally accepted mantra: "It's about learning, always about learning, and only about learning. Everything else is a distant second." Instead, Comer puts student learning into a larger framework that assumes schools must be concerned with the whole child if they are to succeed academically. The best way to operationalize this concern is through the "developmental pathways" that Comer proposes. The pathways are central to Gompers's mission:

> Home-School-Community collaboration ensures that our students have the skills to become contributing members of a global society. Our school will successfully educate all students in a clean, safe, and healthy learning environment. We will meet the needs of the whole child through the developmental pathways: cognitive-intellectual, physical, social-interactive, speech and language, moral, and psycho-emotional [Samuel Gompers Elementary School, 2000, p. 9].

As the Gompers community sees it, "Our goal is to provide a comprehensive school program that improves academic learning and addresses the social, psychological, and emotional development of our children. . . . Our staff ensures that our students' needs are met through a collaborative effort that seeks to address the development of the whole child. . . . A major component of this program is to meet the needs of children through the development pathways" (Samuel Gompers Elementary School, 2000, p. 10). The developmental pathways are briefly described by Gompers's faculty in Exhibit 4.1.

Exhibit 4.1. Developmental Pathways at Gompers Elementary

A major component of this program is to meet the needs of the children through the development pathways: cognitive-intellectual, physical, speech and language, psycho-emotional, moral, and social-interactive. For example, we address the physical pathway (health, nutrition, and fitness) of the children in numerous ways. Hungry children learn at a slower rate . . . therefore 100 percent of our students begin the day with breakfast in their classrooms. There is a supply of clothing, socks, underwear, coats, hats, and gloves readily available to all in need. In 1998 the U.S. Post Office supplied new coats to 75 percent of our students. Before the fifth-grade promotion ceremony the staff makes sure that if a child cannot afford a *new* outfit, one is purchased. A washer and dryer are on-site to take care of clothing emergencies. Last year our full-time school nurse coordinated 154 immunizations, 39 lead screenings, 108 dental cleanings, 205 vision and hearing screenings, and an Asthma Open-Airways Program for 12 children. We provide all students with a "Safe Route" map, so that they all travel the safest path to and from school. Fifteen safety patrol students and two adult crossing guards are strategically placed along this route.

The speech and language pathway (receptive and expressive language and ability to process communications) is addressed daily by our speech therapist, morning assembly, and annual school productions. In a unique intervention program, we invite parents with two- and three-year-old children to speech and language workshops. Over the past five years 60 families have participated in this program. To meet the needs of the psycho-emotional pathway (feelings of adequacy, ability to show emotions, and acceptance of differences) we organize student groups. Some of these groups are intervention programs while others are enrichment programs for the gifted and talented. Since 1996 the numbers of children who have participated in the groups are as follows: 30 in Living with ADHD; 40 in Anger Management; 60 in dance; 65 in art; and 300 in drama. Examples of moral pathway programs (respect for rights and integrity of oneself and others), which address character development, are self-esteem groups, safety patrol, service squad, and Efficacy. Efficacy is a weekly curriculum class for third, fourth, and fifth grade that empowers children to make responsible choices based on their own interest, while respecting the rights and integrity of others.

Exhibit 4.1. Developmental Pathways at Gompers Elementary (continued)

The social-interactive pathway (ability to be empathetic, ability to use communication in relationships, and ability to interact with others who may be different) is covered by our championship basketball team, track team, student-run bagel sale, peer mentoring, and cross-age reading buddies. In the classroom, children read together in pairs during METRA Phonics companion reading. They work in cooperative learning groups to write their stories, solve critical-thinking problems, and perform hands-on experiments. The last pathway, cognitive-intellectual (flexibility of thoughts, ability to manipulate information, and ability to manipulate the environment), has numerous activities associated with it, such as hands-on instruction, METRA Phonics, and basic metacognition techniques. Children can also join the Science Club, the Academic Games Team, and after-school tutoring. Last year 33 percent of our student population attended after-school tutoring. Children are also expected to attend the district-mandated Summer Learning Academy if they have not met the criteria to pass to the next grade in the fall. These programs mentioned are only some of the opportunities and special programs that have been designed to meet students' strengths and weaknesses. One hundred percent of our children benefit from one or more of these programs as documented by our student participation profiles [pp. 10–11].

This [Comer] school improvement process significantly changed the way in which we operate. A child-centered curriculum was designed. Every program was evaluated based on achievement data and the developmental pathways. Programs that did not meet these standards were eliminated and research began on effective program strategies. The School Improvement Team (SIT) became the major decision-making body. In the beginning, we struggled as we made changes. New staff members are now selected by a team, and we make sure that they share our philosophy and vision. Comer gave us an organizational structure and method to make decisions where all voices are heard. This creates ownership in the school program and the understanding that we all have to work together to improve student achievement. Teachers no longer teach in isolation. They meet weekly by grade level and regularly across grade levels. This improves the continuity of curriculum. Now, when we look at how to allocate funds, we examine the developmental pathways and analyze where our money is going and if it needs to be redistributed.

Exhibit 4.1. Developmental Pathways at Gompers Elementary (continued)

In the past, major decisions were made by the principal. These decisions are now being made by the SIT. These decisions are data-driven and based on the needs of our students. We implemented a morning assembly as a result of this process [p. 32].

Source: Samuel Gompers Elementary School, 2000, pp. 10–11, 32. Used with permission of the Detroit Public Schools.

The magic of hope at Gompers is closely linked to faith that certain ideas and assumptions are true and will work if obstacles are identified and overcome. Members of the Gompers community, for example, have high hopes for the academic success of their students. Thanks to the Comer process they have faith in a set of principles that guides their actions. They combine this faith with the belief that, for better or for worse, students react to situations they find themselves in. If you want to change their motivation, attitudes, or behavior, you need to change the situations they are in. In addition, the developmental pathways that the Comer process provides are practical and successful means to change situations. Faith in these ideas makes people hopeful. At Gompers hope has become a reality. Clearly teacher leadership was an important factor in this success. But wise leadership from the principal, Marilee Bylsma, was critical too. Wise leaders are important bearers of hope. They know that hopefulness can provide the margin of encouragement, the margin of clear thinking, and the margin of informed action that make difficult situations manageable and challenging goals attainable.

Some Evidence

Standardized tests alone are not the best indicators of a school's success, but they do tell us something. Gompers students take the Metropolitan Achievement Test (MAT) and the state's Michigan Educational Assessment. Table 4.1 shows examples of test results in reading and math for the years 1995–2000. The source for this test data was the school's winning 2000–2001 Blue Ribbon Award Application. Note that for the Michigan Educational Assessment the percentages of students at or above proficiency for all schools in the City of Detroit are also provided.

Gompers ranked 221 based on the Michigan Educational Assessment scores for 2,013 Michigan schools. Scores aside, Gompers earned the 1996 National Title I School Recognition Award given by the U.S. Department of Education for outstanding progress in compensatory education and was listed in 1995 as one of the ten best schools in Detroit. Among Comer schools nationwide, Gompers is considered to be a model. Turning hope into reality at Gompers gives hope to other schools also struggling to do their best for their students.

Table 4.1. Composite and Gompers Test Scores

Metropolitan Achievement Test—Total composite:
vocabulary and comprehension

Total Composite Scores	1999–2000	1998–1999	1997–1998	1996–1997	1995–1996
1st Grade Reading	68.2	57.6	53.0	59.9	47.2
3rd Grade Reading	80.2	78.4	67.0	53.9	70.0
4th Grade Reading	86.4	78.4	72.0	62.6	69.6

Michigan Educational Assessment—Percentage of Gompers
students and Detroit City students at or above proficiency

Scores	1999–2000	1998–1999	1997–1998	1996–1997	1995–1996
Gompers 4th Grade Reading	100	79	87	87	92
Detroit 4th Grade Reading	52	45	53	47	47
Gompers 4th Grade Math	100	100	100	76	70
Detroit 4th Grade Math	62	59	65	49	49

Hopeful Leadership

In the Preface of this book, the concepts of lifeworld and systemsworld were introduced. Leadership is concerned with the lifeworld and the systemsworld of schools (Sergiovanni, 2000). The lifeworld asks, What are our purposes? Do they reflect what we believe? Are our lifeworld concerns responsive to the needs of students, the needs of teachers, and the needs of other groups? Systemsworld concerns are different: How do we achieve our purposes? What strategies should we develop? How effective are our strategies? What assessments do we need? In this context the lifeworld is the essence of hope. The systemsworld is the means to achieve hope—and both are necessary for the school to succeed. Hope is strengthened by achieving and maintaining proper balance between the lifeworld and the systemsworld. And achieving this balance is an important purpose of leadership. Without it, hope is replaced by wishful thinking.

The Virtue of Trust

Leaders should be trustworthy, and this worthiness is an important virtue. Without trust leaders lose credibility. This loss poses difficulties to leaders as they seek to call people to respond to their responsibilities. The painful alternative is to be punitive, seeking to control people through manipulation or coercion. But trust is a virtue in other ways too. The building of trust is an organizational quality. Once trust exists in a school, it becomes a norm that sets the standard for how teachers, for example, should behave toward each other, toward their students, and toward the school itself. Once embedded in the culture of the school, trust works to liberate people to be their best, to give others their best, and to take risks. All of these are behaviors that help schools become better places for students.

The concept of relational trust was introduced in Chapter Three. It was pointed out that both social capital and relational trust are the DNA of community. They are so integral to the concept of community that operational definitions of community routinely include them. How relational trust became the basis for establishing reciprocal role relationships was also discussed in Chapter Three. Bryk and Schneider noted that "Each party in a role relationship maintains an understanding of his or her role obligations and holds some expectations about the role obligations of others" (2002, p. 20). When trust is abundant, "Teachers feel obligated to work in a professionally appropriate manner and are willing to commit extra effort, if necessary, in seeking to respond to the parents' expectations. Parents in turn are obligated to make sure that students attend school regularly and, more generally, to support the teachers' efforts at home" (pp. 20–21). Without trust these reciprocal bonds of obligation are broken, hampering chances for schools to succeed.

Trust deficits have serious consequences for schools that seem to worsen over time. For example:

- The less trust there is in a school the more people keep things to themselves.

  The more people keep to themselves the less trust there is.

- The less trust there is in a school the more often are ideas hoarded.

  The more often are ideas hoarded the less trust there is.

- The less trust there is in a school the less likely are people to be helpful and open.

  The less likely that people are to be helpful and open, the less trust there is.

Bryk and Schneider (2003) found that relational trust was an important characteristic of schools they studied that demonstrated improvements in student learning. They measured relational trust in terms of teacher attitudes toward other teachers, principals, and parents. They found on average that the improving schools showed an 8 percent increase in reading learning and a 20 percent increase in math learning over five years (p. 43).

Trust First

Schools and school districts that are successful in bringing about change use a trust-first approach. And conversely, in schools and school districts that are less effective in bringing about change trust is an afterthought—having been preceded by vision, strategy, and action. Trust gets attention later, once the school or school district gets into trouble. And this happens further down the line. Typically leaders wind up imposing visions and strategies, and this imposition requires increased monitoring of performance.

David Hurst (1984), former executive vice president of Russel-steel Inc. in Canada, explains that *building trust first* and then moving on to vision, strategy, and action changed the way in which decisions were made in his organization. A trust-first approach forces emphasis on open communications focused on who we are and what we believe. This different way of sharing and this different way of working to incorporate the views of others changed the way in which decisions were made. He writes:

> In our previous existence the decisions we made were always backed up by hard information; management was decisive, and that was good. Unfortunately, too few of these "good" decisions ever got implemented. The simple process of making the decision the way we did often set up resistance down the line. As the decision was handed down to consecutive organizational levels, it lost impetus until eventually it was unclear whether the decision was right in the first place.
>
> Now we worry a good deal less about making decisions; they arise as fairly obvious conclusions drawn from

a mass of shared assumptions. It's the assumptions that we spend our time working on [Hurst, 1984, p. 82].

The traditional vision-first approach to strategy development is contrasted with the trust-first approach in the following list:

Vision-First Approach to Strategy Development	*Trust-First Approach to Strategy Development*
1. Set a vision. ↓	1. Establish trust first. ↓
2. Develop a strategy. ↓	2. Set a vision. ↓
3. Move to action. ↓	3. Develop a strategy. ↓
4. Work on trust. ↓	4. Move to action. ↓

5. Monitor performance, increase evaluation of personnel, retrain.	5. Return to vision and strategy to modify in light of
	  a. what works and what doesn't
	  b. what assumptions are valid
	  c. what core values are compromised.

↓	↓
6. Try to mend fences, improve relationships, and get more people on board to improve effectiveness.	6. Use accumulated trust to forge new strategies for improving effectiveness.

A trust-first approach to strategy development and implementation does not mean that it is necessary to get everybody on board before implementation. There is a "tipping point" that must be respected, and one needs to at least cultivate enough support to trigger it. But in many cases reaching this tipping point does not require that a huge majority must favor the change. In all cases, however, the secret to change is to make sure that everyone has the support and the capacity they need to implement the change successfully. Once someone is successful, and with trust in place, then that person is likely to accept the change and even to like it. As Fullan tells us, "In many cases, changes in behavior precede rather than follow changes in belief" (1991, p. 91). Trust plays an important role in this process. All of us are vulnerable when trying something new, and we need to be assured that mistakes will be accepted and that support will be there.

Bryk and Schneider (2003) found that principals played key roles in developing trust. "Principals establish both respect and personal regard when they acknowledge the vulnerabilities of others, actively listen to their concerns, and eschew arbitrary actions. Effective principals couple these behaviors with a compelling school vision and behavior that clearly seeks to advance the vision. This consistency between words and actions affirms their personal integrity. Then, if the principal competently manages basic day to day school affairs, an overall ethos conducive to the formation of trust will emerge" (p. 43). By paying attention from the start to personal integrity and other dimensions of trust, linking this trust to purposes, providing competent management support, and emphasizing capacity building, principals create conditions for change and people feel more willing to give change a try. These conditions are created when principals work on trust first and then link the trust they create to vision, strategy, and action. Their less effective counterparts, it seems, get around to trust after they encounter resistance—and by then it is usually too late.

Subsidiarity and Mutuality

Two additional virtues can help build trust in schools, subsidiarity and mutuality. These values can be expressed as principles. The principle of *subsidiarity* states that every member of every society and every institution in that society should be free from excessive intervention, circumscription, or regulation by the state or any other larger institution (see, for example, Hollenbach, 1995; Starratt, 1996). This principle places faith and responsibility in local rights and initiatives. In schools, what students, teachers, parents, and local administrators stand for and believe should be done counts and they know it. Those closest to the principal's office, the classroom, and the home, for example, are presumed to be in the best position to decide whether a student should be promoted or not. Though higher levels have a right to provide policies, these policies should not replace the judgment of principals, parents, and teachers. Empowerment of this kind, when coupled with the reciprocal role responsibilities discussed in Chapter Three, builds trust.

The principle of *mutuality* states that interdependence in the form of mutually beneficial associations characterized by dignity and respect among people, among different institutions, and between different levels of government should characterize their relationships (see, for example, Nothwehr, 1998). This principle, too, places faith and responsibility in local rights and initiatives but sees them as integral parts of a larger community where interests from all levels of this larger community come together on an equal footing. Mutuality depends upon a level of intimacy between the elements that is characterized by trust and respect. Mutuality also depends upon parity. When people are brought together in a school under the principles of subsidiarity and mutuality, trust grows (Sergiovanni, 2000).

The Virtues of Piety and Civility

Embedded in concepts of community, school as community, learning community, professional community, community of practice, and other variations is a tension that leaders in schools inevitably face. This tension is between the common ties that hold communities together and the rational ties that encourage them to reach out to others. And this is where piety and civility fit in. Ideally piety and civility are complementary virtues. Havoc is raised when piety and civility drift apart. This is because of the norms of self-ishness, competition, calculation, and indifference that are likely to emerge as a result.

The virtue of piety embodies the showing of loyalty, respect, and affection such as is usually found among friends, comrades in arms, close colleagues at work, and other groups where caring and oblig-ations characterize connections among people. Piety is important in families, churches, neighborhoods, and other social organizations that resemble communities. These organizations provide members with feelings of belonging, a sense of place, deep meaning, identity, and significance. Accompanying piety is relational trust and other virtues that stretch the bonds among people in such a way that they feel obligated to look after each other.

Piety is a conditional leadership virtue when it is applied in cir-cumstances that require or encourage people to look inward to their own narrow community affiliations. This inwardness is usually at the expense of looking outward to more rational and impersonal organizations or groups. As a result, leaders in schools can become blinded to other views. This blindness encourages isolation and exclusiveness that seriously limits their ability to learn from others, to be exposed to new ideas, and to make new friends and meet new colleagues.

The virtue of civility draws us outward to embrace differences at the same time that piety draws us inward toward shared identi-ties. Though piety is an important ingredient in building collabo-rative work cultures, it is as well an important ingredient in gangs and cliques at school that develop special bonds. Looking inward in these cases means to exclude others. By their nature cliques of students or adults wind up being isolated. This can be the case for schools, teams, and departments within schools. When held together by piety alone these schools, teams, or departments become isolated from each other.

As Selznick (2002) explains: "Some forms of piety ask too much of us, and for the wrong objects, or claim immunity from criticism or demand undivided and unconditional loyalty. Therefore, piety is tempered by the more dispassionate virtue of civility. Piety demands conformity and justifies exclusion, while civility welcomes diversity, encourages toleration, and legitimates controversy. Civility builds frameworks within which people can cooperate despite their divergent views and interests" (p. 68).

Bonding and Bridging Community

The virtues of piety and civility together are at the heart of building learning communities that bond people together while creating bridges that connect them to other people and to other views (see, for example, Putnam, 2000).

Effective communities in schools depend upon the virtue of piety to provide a floor of shared values and ideas that ties everyone together, that provides security and support, and that gives the school a special identity that communicates its character and purposes. This "bonding community" is critical. At the same time bridges need to be built among different groups within the school and with different groups outside the school. This "bridging community" honors diversity and provides opportunities for learning as groups are exposed to new ideas. But this balance does not just happen. Schools and their leaders have to work at cultivating the idea of balanced unity so that it becomes a central value within a school's culture.

Bonding community, according to Putnam (2000), "constitutes a kind of sociological superglue." Bridging community, by contrast, "provides a sociological WD-40" (p. 23). Putnam points out:

> Many groups simultaneously bond along some social dimensions and bridge across others. The black church, for example, brings together people of the same race and

religion across class lines. The Knights of Columbus was created to bridge cleavages among different ethnic communities while bonding along religious and gender lines. Internet chat groups may bridge across geography, gender, age, and religion, while being tightly homogeneous in education and ideology. In short, bonding and bridging are not "either-or" categories into which social networks can be neatly divided, but "more or less" dimensions along which we can compare different forms of social capital [p. 23].

Schools, too, bond along some dimensions and bridge across others. A school might bond around shared values and ideas such as a commitment to care, providing rigorous academic learning, believing in the importance of effort, and developing faculty relationships that encourage the sacrificing of self-interest for the common good. At the same time, this school might bridge along other dimensions such as honoring cultural diversity and providing developmentally diverse safety nets for students who are falling behind—safety nets that respond to different student needs and different learning styles in different ways, as in the collective commitments that various constituent groups at Adlai Stevenson High School made to help each of the groups move closer to the school's vision, as described in Chapter Three. These commitments, along with the vision they were intended to reach, are examples of bonding community. The faculty, for example, binds itself to a common set of ideas. As a result, the bonds among them strengthen. But still, different faculty teams are free to decide for themselves exactly how they are going to embody these commitments in their practice. Further, reaching out to other faculty teams to learn how they are doing things and relying on the numerous learning opportunities provided by Stevenson High School provide bridging that not only unites a large and diverse faculty but opens their hearts and minds to new ideas and encourages continuous learning.

One Out of Many

Selznick offers *E pluribus unum* (one out of many) as the metaphor for bringing piety and civility together. "We say yes to plurality even as we uncover convergent truths. A rich variety of beliefs and forms. . . . should be accepted and supported" (2002, p. 72).

On the *unum* side Selznick notes: "Human differences are appreciated most keenly, and welcomed most sincerely, when they testify to an underlying unity. Our common humanity generates diverse ways of life. . . . That same humanity produces cultural universals" (2002, p. 72). In schools, cultural universals include the values, standards, and norms that are meant to be shared by everyone. These cultural universals are accompanied by other values, standards, and norms that are meant to be shared by some but not all. The two sets of values, standards, and norms together create a layered system of loyalty and commitments—a floor of common understandings that supports differences. While all students are expected to dress modestly, they need not all dress the same way. Though students may elect to take a number of courses beyond the common core, all courses must meet the same standards of rigor, student involvement, and usefulness. Teachers are expected to work together in professional development that is tied to grade, team, and department purposes, but they may also choose different topics and venues for learning to suit their own individual needs and interests.

The Gompers Elementary School gets high marks for building the kind of bonding community that pulls everyone together. Though comparatively bridging community does not seem that strong within the school, Gompers excels at building outside bridges with parents and other community groups, as well as with sister Comer schools throughout the country.

Love

It is hard to talk about and to think about leadership virtues without eventually getting around to love. The importance of the virtue *love* in leadership is unofficial. Most school leaders will recognize its value in strengthening the heartbeat of leadership and in building community in schools. But we have virtually no literature on this topic.[2] There is, however, a literature on caring and caring is a cousin to love.

Good evidence exists that caring can help bridge the achievement gap that exists in too many schools. Most often the culprit is connections or their lack. Too many African American and Hispanic students, for example, are not achieving because they are disconnected from schooling. Both Nel Noddings (1992) and Angela Valenzuela (1999) have pointed out that before students can become connected to the school and its work, they must first become connected to a caring adult at school. In Valenzuela's words, "Their precondition to caring about schools is that they engage in a caring relationship with an adult at school" (p. 74).

Love becomes a duty and an obligation when one views school leadership as a vocation or a calling. Love is the basis for the practice of servant leadership. Servant leadership requires that one loves the purposes, goals, and intents that define the leader's work and that of the school. Servant leadership requires that one loves those who are being served.

---

[2] John Hoyle's recent book, *Leadership and the Force of Love* (2002), is a rare exception.

· ·

5

A Teacher-Centered Approach

A teacher-centered approach? Wait a minute. I thought that schools should be student centered. It's "all about the kids." Isn't that what we are supposed to say? A safe guess is that schools should be about both, but with an important corollary: All of the learning and all of the support we want students to experience depends in large measure on the support that teachers receive. This support not only includes the nitty-gritty working conditions of teachers (for example, salary, access to a telephone, adequate materials, time for lunch, a clean and comfortable work environment, respectful students, and discipline policies that work) but the opportunities that teachers have to work together with colleagues, to learn more about their craft, to make important decisions about teaching, learning, and other professional matters. All of these conditions and opportunities count. They count so much that unless we look after them schools will not work as effectively as they can for students. An important truism is that as the principal goes, so goes the school. But the corollary to that statement is also true. As the teacher goes, so goes the student.

Roland Barth's now-famous homily reminding us to heed the advice routinely given by airline cabin attendants at takeoff makes sense: "In the unlikely event that an oxygen mask is needed and you are accompanied by a child, first put the mask on yourself and then on the child." Teachers are best able to serve students when they themselves have been adequately served. But let me back up for a moment and examine the larger picture linking the effects of school-level variables, teacher-level variables, and student-level variables on student achievement.

What Counts

As a result of his research and his analysis of the research of others, Marzano (2000) concludes that school leadership ranks seventh in a field of eight school-level factors that contribute to student achievement. The first six factors, in order, are opportunities for students to learn, amount of time students spend learning, monitoring of student progress, providing a reasonable amount of pressure for students to achieve, parental involvement, and a supportive school climate. Only cooperation was rated lower than leadership. But things may not be as they seem. Leadership plays by different rules. It has, for example, many lives. One of its lives is to stand alone as a factor that contributes directly to student achievement. Its other lives, however, serve to fuel and enhance school-level and teacher-level variables in ways that help these variables influence student achievement.

Marzano (2000) notes, for example, that as a group the school-level variables account for only about 7 percent of the variance influencing student achievement. Teacher-level variables such as instructional strategies, curriculum design, and classroom management accounted for about 13 percent of the variance. Student-level variables—home atmosphere, prior knowledge, and motivation, aptitude, and interest—account for 80 percent of the variance with home atmosphere having the most powerful effect on student achievement.

Compared to student-level variables the effects of school-level and teacher-level variables seem not to count very much. But they do. Marzano notes, for example, that "The finding that schools account for only 10 percent of the differences in student achievement translates into a percentile gain of about 23 points. That is, the average student who attends a 'good' school will have a score that is 23 percentile points higher than the average student who attends a poor school. From this perspective, schools definitely can make a difference in student achievement" (cited in Association for Supervision and Curriculum Development, 2003, p. 1). Still, in a comparative sense, if we assume that leadership has to have direct effects on student achievement to count, then probably it doesn't count much. But if we take the indirect effects leadership has on teachers, students, and school-level variables into account, then we get a different picture. Leadership emerges as a powerful force that provides the conditions and support schools need to succeed and teachers need to be effective. With the right kind of leadership, teacher effects on student achievement are likely to be higher.

In a recent meta-analysis, for example, McREL researchers Waters, Marzano, and McNulty found that "for an average school, having an effective leader can mean the difference between scoring at the 50th percentile on a given achievement test and achieving a score 10 percentile points higher" (Viadero, 2003). The variable making the most difference on a school's test scores was the extent to which the leader understood the details and the undercurrents of running a school and used this knowledge successfully. This effect is indirect. The McREL study is described in more detail in Chapter Eight.

These assertions are supported by a series of authoritative papers written by Hallinger and Heck (1996a, 1996b, 1999). These papers document the importance of principals' indirect leadership in improving student achievement. In short, Hallinger and Heck find that principal leadership does not provide a measurable direct effect but does provide a measurable indirect effect.

In sum, Marzano's work and that of others strongly suggest that leadership is often less visible in practice and thus less likely to show its impact statistically. Nonetheless, leadership is an important precursor to success (Marzano, 2003). Virtually every variable that affects student achievement in schools is itself likely to be affected by leadership. As leadership grows in quality and quantity, school effects and teacher effects grow in robustness, becoming better able to influence student learning and school achievement in positive ways. For this reason, any effort designed to improve teacher quality as a means to increasing student learning must include leadership in its equation. This view is echoed by Kent Peterson, a distinguished researcher at the University of Wisconsin, who has spent twenty years studying the principalship. He concludes "for schools to be effective centers of learning strong principals are critical for shaping the culture and climate" (Peterson, 2002, p. 6).

A Two-Bridge Approach

One of the reasons for the success of Stevenson High School and Gompers Elementary School (see Chapters Four and Six) and for the success of many other schools is their ability to organize around and to successfully use collaborative cultures. These cultures are the backbone of dynamic learning communities that bring leadership and learning together. This joining of the two is the strategy successful schools use for working together day by day, for launching change initiatives, and for continuous improvement.

Scratching the surface of this strategy reveals that schools and districts that have the most success in enhancing student achievement take a two-bridge rather than a one-bridge approach. To understand the difference, it's necessary to think in terms of initiating, mediating, and results variables. Gains in student achievement, for example, are *results* variables. What teachers, administrators, and others actually do in trying to get results are *initiating* variables. In between are the *mediating* variables. These mediating variables respond or react to the initiating variables in ways that enhance results, have no effect on results, or have negative effects on results. In the jargon of research, mediating variables exhibit indirect causation.

Principals and teachers, for example, might take learning walks together or principals might manipulate schedules to allow teachers more opportunities to visit each other's classrooms and to share lesson plans with each other (initiating variables). If teachers learn more as a result and develop stronger collegial ties with each other (mediating variables), they are more likely to be successful in improving student achievement (results variables). If principals create schedules that encourage teacher isolation, we might get a negative reaction and less effective teaching and learning.

The message for strategy here is that if you want positive results, calibrate your leadership in a fashion that is aimed at changing the mediating variables for the good. If you have been successful, then the mediating variables will do their work in improving student learning. In contrast, trying to directly link what principals, superintendents, and other leaders do to student achievement (going from initiating variables directly to results variables, thus ignoring mediating variables) is like "trying to paint a portrait with a brush a yard long."[1] In sum, we can choose a one-bridge or two-bridge approach as follows:

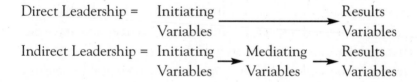

The one-bridge approach seeks to directly influence student achievement results. But the "single span" between the two seems to lack the proper supports for change. Further, the distance between initiating variables and results variables is too long for leaders to accurately read the situational and contextual issues they face and to accurately respond accordingly. And finally, those leaders who are at the initiating variable end often lack the technical knowledge to positively influence results in a direct way. What they know how to do is to enhance the mediating variables. They know how to build strong, focused, and helpful learning cultures,

[1] Attributed to Tom Sobol.

how to provide opportunities for teachers to lead, how to move expertness around the school so that it is in the right place at the right time, how to listen to others, how to help build confidence, how to teach the school's culture to newcomers, how to repeat and repeat what the school is about, how to use the school's idea structure as a source of authority for what is done in the school, how to manipulate schedules so that they are teacher-learning friendly, how to engage in learning walks to ensure that shared ideas are being embodied in classrooms, how to take over a classroom for a couple of hours so that the teacher can help a colleague who is having a problem, and how to share leadership with others when they are entitled to have it.

Thus, the two-bridge approach focuses more deliberately and with more precision on what leaders actually do and what effect their actions have on such things as developing collaborative cultures, enhancing student learning, building a covenantal community, providing in-class and on-the-job professional development experiences, working on ensuring a safe environment characterized by caring and respect, providing the resources and amenities that teachers need not only to work more effectively but to view their jobs more favorably. As these mediating variables and the others described in the preceding paragraph increase, so will student-learning results increase.

What About Students?

How do students fit into this equation? Where are the student concerns within the mediating variables? If a principal's attention is not directly on students, then how can the school be a student-centered place? It probably can't if we looked at things in the same way. But if we can see that student-centeredness is *embedded within* teacher-centeredness, then not being student centered in a direct way may be a plus. A hyper-student-centered school, one where all that matters is student achievement and all of our efforts are concentrated on this goal, simply will not work over time anyway. Focusing on the mediating variables helps us make the school more of a teacher-centered place first and this may be a better strategy. Once the school achieves this goal then teachers will be better able to serve students and desired results will be achieved.

To be teacher centered first is to place a high priority on helping teachers learn, helping them to be more successful in the classroom, helping them to be more committed to school standards and values, to find their jobs intellectually stimulating, to be able to collaborate with colleagues, to find sense and meaning in their work, to be more committed to self-supervision and self-evaluation, to be more receptive to other forms of accountability, and to help teachers be more effective instructional leaders. Teacher-centeredness also means that teachers need a respectful place to work, decent working conditions, better pay, and more discretion to make better decisions for their students. And finally, a teacher-centered approach acknowledges the link between teacher quality and student learning in both its talk and action (see Table 5.1 at the end of this chapter for a summary of recent studies that link teacher quality with student achievement). As Lieberman and Miller (1999) see it: "The strong connection between students' learning and teachers' workplace conditions cannot be ignored. In schools that do not find the balance, trouble looms ahead. In schools that focus primarily on teachers' workplace conditions, the outside community often responds, 'What does all this have to do with the children?' In schools that focus primarily on students' learning, teachers often feel overwhelmed and under appreciated." (p. 12). And further, "If change is to have meaning, it must be related to students and their success in schools; and it must acknowledge the needs and concerns of teachers as they change the way they work" (p. 11).

Providence as an Example

Since 2000, Providence, Rhode Island, has been involved in a districtwide initiative to improve its schools.[2] Providence provides an example of how inescapable a teacher-centered approach is to any school improvement effort that includes increasing levels of student achievement. Providence's plan, *Rekindling the Dream*, has three major goals:

- Improve student achievement results by focusing on teaching and learning with teachers playing key roles

- Build capacity among the faculty for continuous learning

- Strengthen parent involvement

To achieve these goals, Anderson and Togneri (2003) note, Providence adopted five core strategies:

1. Create a common focus for improvement.

2. Build school-level leadership capacity.

3. Hold leaders accountable for results.

4. Emphasize professional development over curriculum development.

5. Create a balance between central direction and site-based needs.

The Stealth Quality of Leadership

Each of the strategies seeks to help Providence achieve its student learning goals, but none of the strategies involve a direct link between leadership and student achievement. The first strategy that

---

[2] The primary source for this discussion is Steven Anderson and Wendy Togneri's 2003 paper, "Building Instructional Leadership: A Case Study of the Providence Public School Department." Initial leadership for the Providence reform effort was given by Diana Lam, who served as superintendent from 1999 through 2002. Melody Johnson has been at the helm since. I am grateful to Superintendent Johnson, Mary Kay Schnare, and all the Providence principals and "aspiring principals" I met in the fall of 2002 for insight into how things work in Providence. At root, the Providence approach is based on the work of Lauren Resnick and her colleagues at the Institute for Learning in Pittsburgh. Key to her work was the identification of nine principles of learning and the development of strategies for their implementation. Many of Resnick's ideas were initially developed and tested in New York City's District 2 during the Anthony Alvarado and Elaine Fink years. The nine principles of learning appear in Chapter Seven.

sought to improve the effectiveness of schools (results variables) was led by the central office and aimed at developing a school system with a focus on student performance, particularly in the area of literacy (initiating variables). The intent was to help teachers be more competent and confident and to increase their commitment to reform efforts (mediating variables). The second strategy sought to improve the instructional leadership capacity of principals and teachers at the building level by adopting a "distributed leadership" perspective that sought to share leadership with central office, principals, and teachers in areas where they were best suited to influence results. The theory here being that as leadership capacity builds, teaching and learning effectiveness increases and student achievement will rise.

The third strategy, being accountable for results, was particularly important. "District leaders spoke of 'two-way accountability' between teachers and principals, principals and district office personnel such that all parties were mutually accountable for carrying out their respective responsibilities" (Anderson and Togneri, 2003, p. 5). This strategy relied on the resurrection of reciprocal role relationships—the establishment of rights and obligations that link two roles together; and the resurrection of role sets—bundles of role relationships that represent friendly networks of individuals linked together by mutual expectations, rights, and responsibilities (see Chapter Three). Thinking in terms of roles and talking about reciprocal rights and responsibilities leads to the principles of subsidiarity and mutuality discussed in Chapter Four. The first principle places faith and responsibility in local rights and initiatives. And the second requires levels of intimacy characterized by trust and respect. Mutuality also depends upon parity. Both principles are champions of a more teacher-centered environment for schools.

The fourth strategy, emphasizing professional development over curriculum development, shifted the focus away from developing curriculum toward understanding and using the new state standards. In part the intent was to create a new instructional coherence that let students know what is expected of them and that forged learning networks of teachers who work together on how to help students reach the standards. Without intensive professional development support this strategy would merely exchange one script (the required scope and sequence) for another (the required standards). Together teachers worked on the standards, developed and shared lesson plans that were aligned with the standards, and developed common assessments. The professional development focus was on both "what would I like to learn or what should I be learning given my strengths and weaknesses" and "what must all of us be learning and learning together in order to more effectively prepare students for success." Again, teachers were placed at the center. And district investment in their learning was viewed as a key to success.

The fifth strategy, balancing central direction with school-based needs, broadened the context within which teachers usually live in schools. If this "balancing" was one way with the district providing mandates and oversight for aligning professional development with literacy goals, then teachers would remain on the bottom of the heap, required to do what they were told to do. But if this balancing was the way the central office and school would forge new partnerships for mutual learning and support, then we would have a different result. Providence sought the latter approach, recognizing that all district priorities needed to be adjusted and adopted to student-level needs and to the needs of teachers who were working in specific contexts and situations. The district was committed, for example, to a school-based, job-embedded approach to professional development that prized collegiality not just in the school but beyond. Teachers were at the center of emergent communities of practice that included consultants from the central office, principals, and even the superintendent herself—a strategy that honored teachers and their learning.

Clearly Providence is not the only district in America to recognize more and more that student-centeredness works best when it is embedded in a culture that prizes teachers and their learning.

Deep and Lasting Improvement

Susan Fuhrman (2003) argues that reform may be the wrong metaphor for gauging changes that matter in schools—changes that actually affect teaching and learning in a deep and sustained way. We have tried reform, she notes. We have reorganized schools in various and seemingly endless configurations as if we were preoccupied with structure—with changing the way things look in schools but not improving the results that schools are getting. In her words:

> So, if "reform" is not the answer, what is? Perhaps we need to shift the metaphor from "reform" to "improvement." Reform is a matter of policies swooping down from on high. Improvement is a matter of continued attention to the basics of teaching and learning—the heart of schooling. Improvement is slow, unending, not particularly glamorous, hard work. It involves deep investment in teacher quality and knowledge, through recruiting, compensating, and developing teachers. It involves thoughtful, well-funded professional development that is intensive, extensive (over a period of time), focused on the curriculum that teachers are teaching, and followed up by coaching and other on-site support [p. 10].

Teacher quality is important, and recent efforts to reform schools by emphasizing teacher learning and the development of professional learning communities are helpful. But are they helpful enough to trigger the turnaround needed to make schools intellectual environments for teachers and students and to result in deep and long-lasting improvements? Cohen and Sheer (2003) say no. Deep and lasting improvements will be achieved, they argue, only when teachers are placed at the center of attention and when everyone else and everything else is placed at the periphery. Though students and parents, testing and accountability policies, and bureaucratic and managerial requirements have important roles to play in schooling, teachers should be at the center. As Cohen and Sheer see it, improvement will happen when schools are redefined as intellectual centers. Cohen (2002) states, for example, "For a school to be an intellectual center, for it to have the ethos, the sense of community, and the 'spirit' that so many parents and administrators seek, it must celebrate the work of its teachers in a way that is rarely seen in public schools. It must attend to the needs of teachers, it must accommodate their sensibilities, and it must treat the teachers' contributions with as much genuine concern as it does those of any other constituency" (p. 533).

Cohen and Sheer's views are echoed by Bunting (2003) as follows:

> Experts do much good, but when they are used as stand-ins for the thinking teachers must do for themselves, damage is done. This is because the important work of the teacher really is to think about teaching, to think about it all day, every day, and through the thinking to get better at the doing. No new program can achieve this for teachers, no new theory, no latest fix. The work is just too complex to be captured this simply. The work has its own way—a slow, hard, and persistent way that is best described as "mindfulness". . . . But mindfulness goes deeper. It digs into the nooks and crannies of all school life, drawing strength from the intellectual context teachers build for themselves and for one another. Formal learning helps: the workshops teachers attend, the conferences they go to, the advanced degrees they earn. But the layering of a school's intellectual context is far more intricate, far less amenable to planning and scheduling. It builds from questions teachers raise as they talk in hallways. It grows from practices observed as another's and wisely adopted as one's own. It feeds significantly from stories teachers tell one another about teaching, and thrives on helpful advice and shared confidences between teachers [p. 41].

The arguments of Cohen, Sheer, and Bunting are compelling enough to deserve careful consideration and broad discussion—but are we giving away the store? Are not there dangers in placing teachers at the center? Is it a good idea to redistribute power in this way? Wouldn't principals and superintendents, their boards and parents have less say? After all, teacher-centeredness may not be as altruistic as Cohen, Sheer, and Bunting say.

These are valid concerns. But informed opinion suggests that empowering teachers, supporting their work, and improving their working conditions does not dilute but thickens the amount of power and authority that is available for everyone else. Think back to the work of Arnold Tannenbaum (1968), summarized in Chapter Two. Tannenbaum found that designated leaders such as principals and other administrators actually increased their control over achieving school purposes by giving up power. Further, he noted that the total amount of power that existed across ranks in an organization was a better predictor of both satisfaction and performance than was the relative amount of power held by one group (administrators, for example) as compared with another group (teachers and students, for example).

Accountability

The bottom line is that principals, superintendents, and boards are accountable for ensuring that schools are not only effective but keep getting better. It is deep and lasting improvement that the public wants. If teachers are able to work more productively at teaching and learning, principals, superintendents, and boards are going to be more successful. If teachers are not able to work more productively, then schools will not be as effective as they must be. A teacher-centered approach, so it seems, helps everyone become a winner at the game of accountability for effective teaching and learning. Teachers get the support they need to be successful. Students learn more. And the schools' leadership measures up to the public's demands.

Table 5.1. Teacher Quality and Student Achievement: A Summary of Recent Research

In his study of nine hundred Texas teachers, Ferguson found that teacher expertise as measured by scores on licensing examinations accounted for 40 percent of the variation in reading and writing achievement for students in Grades 1–11. Teacher expertise was more important than any other factor. Ferguson noted that every dollar spent on enhancing teacher quality resulted in greater student achievement than did investing that same dollar in other factors.	Ferguson, R. "Paying for Public Education: New Evidence on How and Why Money Matters." *Harvard Journal on Legislation,* Summer 1991, 28(2), 465–498.
After reviewing the research, Linda Darling-Hammond concluded that while demographic characteristics are related to student achievement, they are not as influential in predicting student achievement as are quality of teacher variables.	Darling-Hammond, L. "Teacher Quality and Student Achievement: A Review of State Policy Evidence." *Educational Policy Analysis Archives,* 2000, 8(1), 1–50.
Steven Rivkin and Eric Hanushek found that when compared with least-effective teachers, more-effective teachers managed to get one additional year's worth of learning from their students. Research in Texas, for example, found that having a very good teacher instead of an average teacher for four years in a row could close the achievement gap in math between high-income and low-income students.	Rivkin, S., and Hanushek, E. Cited in "To Close the Gap, Quality Counts." *Education Week,* Jan. 9, 2003, p. 10.

William Sanders and Sandra Horn concluded that differences in achievement between students with high-quality teachers for three consecutive years and students with low-quality teachers for the same period was 50 percentile points on standardized tests.

S. Paul Wright, Sandra Horn, and William Sanders note, "The immediate and clear implication . . . is that seemingly more can be done to improve education by improving the effectiveness of teachers than by any other single factor" (p. 63).

Teachers' knowledge of subject matter influences student performance. Teachers with proper training in the subjects they teach had students who achieved more.

"Having good teachers is the single most important factor in providing a good education for kids. Research shows that students of the best teachers learn up to six times more than students of less effective teachers."

Sanders, W. L., and Horn, S. P. "The Tennessee Value-Added Assessment System (TVAAS) Mixed-Model Methodology in Educational Assessment." *Journal of Personnel Evaluation in Education*, 1994, 8, 299–311.

Wright, S. P., Horn, S., and Sanders, W. "Teacher and Classroom Context Effects on Student Achievement: Implications for Teacher Evaluation." *Journal of Personnel Evaluation in Education*, 1997, 11(1), 57–67.

"To Close the Gap, Quality Counts." *Education Week*, Jan. 9, 2003, p. 10.

Puriefoy, W. "Newsblast Special Edition: Give Kids Good Schools." *Public Education Network*, Jan. 7, 2003.

6

. . . .

Collaborative Cultures and Organizational Competence

In most schools teaching is regarded as an individual practice. Thirty teachers working in the same school are thought of as a collection of thirty individual practices. This is the way the profession of teaching has been set up and the way it seems to work virtually everywhere. This reality is in strong contrast to what is found in most other professions. The reason for concern is simple: "Competence in any organization can rarely be traced to a single individual. Organizational competence typically resides in the relationships, norms, memories, habits, and collective skills of a network of people" (Wilkins, 1989, p. 41). Organizational competence is the sum of everything everybody knows and uses that leads to increased learning (see, for example, Stewart, 1997). This competence is measured not only by what we know but by how much of it we know, how widely it is distributed, how broad its source is, how much of it is applied collectively, and how much of it is generated by cooperation with others. Organizational competence strengthens the heartbeat of leadership.

Too often competence is divided among different people. The consequence of this division is to dilute what each individual knows and to ignore the collective intelligence that schools might otherwise have. Without this collective intelligence, it is doubtful that closing the achievement gap and resolving other intractable problems will ever become more than wishful thinking.

The problem, as Jacob Bronowski (1978) sees it, is that while many professions have evolved into communities where competence multiplies because it is aggregated, other professions have not. He uses science as an example:

> I want to turn your attention now to the community of scientists. Because you see, what has made science successful as a social leaven over the last three hundred years is its change from the practice of individuals, however great their ingenuity, to a communal enterprise. Leonardo da Vinci was born in 1452. He died in 1519. No scientific society existed at that time. . . . And one reason why immensely prolific, vivid, imaginative, and inventive brains like Leonardo's failed to make any impact on the body of science was that there were no colleagues. There were colleagues in painting, and they undoubtedly had an influence which produced more and better paintings than we should otherwise have . . . even that tremendous mind could not work in isolation [pp. 122–123].

Da Vinci was much more successful at painting than he was at science. At the time there existed a powerful community of painters and only a fledgling community of scientists. In da Vinci's case the accumulated competence of the first overwhelmed the competence of the second.

Collaborative cultures are indeed powerful. But as with most things, we need to be cautious in advocating the development of collaborative cultures in schools if the result is the neglect of the virtues of individualism. Relying on Fullan (1991), Robert Evans (1996) points out that though our present interest in collaborative cultures is appealing, it may overlook a fundamental advantage of teachers' working alone. Autonomy may be threatened in the first instance but could thrive in the second. Thus we do not want a good-versus-bad dichotomy. Instead, we want a careful and considered balance that increases the competence of the school without unduly decreasing the amount of autonomy that people have. Huberman notes, "Separateness has its costs, but it offers the benefits of freedom, benefits so rewarding that they have created an 'ecosystem' among teachers that is exceptionally 'complex, coherent, and resilient' with an 'awesome capacity to wait out and wear out reformers'" (Huberman, 1993, p. 44, as cited in Evans, 1996, p. 241).

If we are successful in introducing such practices as leadership as entitlement, using ideas as the primary source of authority for leadership and introducing conditions that lead to teachers' gathering as communities of practice, norms of isolation will be replaced by norms of collegiality. This change will take more than wishful thinking and more than having the right vision. This change will require the development of action strategies and norms of behavior that come from public declarations of commitment to what constituent groups need to do. This change will require lots of follow-up by principals and other designated leaders.

When collaborative cultures work, everyone in the school is part of a role that defines each individual's obligations and everyone is part of a reciprocal role relationship that spells out mutual obligations. Reciprocal role relationships exist within role sets that are the seeds for the bubbling up of informal communities of practice in a school and the trickling down of institutionalized collaborative cultures. When informal communities of practice become part of institutionalized collaborative cultures, we find the balance we need between individual autonomy and collaborative work.

Collaboration at Adlai Stevenson High School

One school that has struck the right balance between individual autonomy and collaborative cultures is Adlai Stevenson High School in Lincolnshire, Illinois.[1] Consider, for example, how

[1] Thanks to Principal Dan Galloway of Adlai Stevenson High School, to teachers Stephanie Neuberger and Carol Levin, and to Director John Carter of the Math Division for sharing their thoughts with me. I appreciate, also, the help received from Richard DuFour, who was a long-time principal and superintendent at Stevenson. Thanks also to Eric Twadell, the Social Studies Division director.

Stephanie Neuberger, a new teacher at Stevenson, describes her experiences at being hired.

> My first impression of Stevenson's hiring process was that it is incredibly thorough. I met my director, Eric, at a large job fair held at a nearby college campus. Two days later I received a phone call from Eric inviting me to visit the high school to observe for a day to see if Stevenson was a school I could see myself working in.
>
> Eric met me outside the principal's office and immediately made me feel welcome. On the way to his office, Eric introduced me to two first-year teachers who were at their desks as we were walking by. Both seemed very friendly and interested in meeting me. Once inside Eric's office, Eric explained that he wanted me to spend the morning observing in various social studies classrooms and that we would meet again in the afternoon to discuss my experience. Eric assigned a teacher, Laura, to guide me from one classroom to another for the morning.
>
> That morning, I observed in four different classrooms and began to get a better idea of what Stevenson's culture includes. Although each of the teachers I observed that morning had vastly different styles of teaching, they all shared a few commonalities, namely, an obvious passion for their subject, and a sense of truly caring about their students. In each of the classrooms was a high level of excitement and energy that I wanted to be a part of.
>
> I also had the chance to speak with each of the teachers during the passing periods and each had more positive things to say than the previous teacher. I really got the impression that these teachers enjoyed coming to work each day. This group of teachers had relationships with their colleagues that transcended just a working relationship—they were friends.

Eric and I then spent the next class period talking about my impressions of the school and answering one another's questions. At the end of our meeting, Eric invited me back for another interview. He gave me a copy of the Social Studies Department's Vision Statement and told me to read it over and become familiar with it before the next interview. He also told me that the interview would be a panel interview and to expect a group of people asking questions as opposed to just him. I was really thankful that Eric was so clear about what to expect in the next interview.

About one month later the interview took place. This time, the meeting was in the administration office and was much more formal. Eric walked me into the conference room and introduced me to the panel. Immediately I was put at ease (at least as "at ease" as one can feel during an interview) because I recognized two of the interviewers, Laura and Laurie. I really felt like I had clicked with both these teachers the month before during my visit to the school so I was very happy to see them as part of the interview panel.

Once seated, I was offered a cookie and something to drink. I declined because I was too nervous to eat and I was terrified I might spill something on one of the people who was interviewing me. The people conducting the interview seemed as though they were trying to do everything they could to make me feel at ease. They smiled when I was answering questions and at times voiced sentiments of agreement.

The final step was having Eric visit the school where I was student teaching and observe me teach a lesson. I was very nervous about the visit, but Eric immediately put me at ease. Prior to the observation, Eric met with the two teachers I was student teaching under and heard a bit from them about my progress. I was happy that he met with them because I knew then that even if I royally messed up, he would have heard some positive feedback about the job I was doing.

After his observation, Eric and I met and talked about the class period that he had watched. We spent a few minutes debriefing the lesson and talking about what worked and what could be changed in the future. In hindsight I can see the value of Eric asking me my opinion; my guess is that he was looking to see if I had the ability to reflect upon my teaching style. Next, Eric described the opening that he had to see if it was something I would be interested in. After hearing his description of the job, I knew that I was interested and accepted the job.

I began to learn more about Stevenson's culture that summer. One of the subjects I would be teaching was Advanced Placement Psychology, so the AP Psychology team had a few meetings to discuss curriculum and methods of teaching. The unbelievable amount of support and guidance I received over the course of the school year was foreshadowed by the events of the summer. During the summer months and thereafter the other AP Psychology teachers, Laura and Laurie, walked me through how to teach the course on a day-by-day basis.

A key element of the Stevenson culture, as I see it, is the strong relationships between administrators and teachers, teachers with other teachers, and of course teachers with students. The first two types of relationships began over the summer months prior to classes beginning. The first year of teaching is always going to be marked by challenges, but the added pressure of teaching an Advanced Placement course added another layer. In some ways, I found teaching AP easier than teaching regular because of all the help I received. Laura and Laurie both helped me master the content along with how to forge positive relationships with students. They were a great support system and helped to keep me grounded at times when I otherwise would have felt very overwhelmed. It is this type of relationship that makes me feel so lucky to be teaching at Stevenson [Stephanie Neuberger, personal communication, June 2003].

Stephanie's story is a remarkable example of how important being teacher centered first is to schools that value teaching and learning. To be successful, Stevenson realizes that authentic student-centeredness requires that concern for students and their learning be embedded in a culture that values teachers, invests in their learning, and encourages their professionalism.

Stephanie's experiences with selection at Stevenson suggest that the Social Studies Department (and other departments at Stevenson) is both a community of practice and a collaborative culture at the same time. Communities of practice bubble up as teachers voluntarily support each other's practice by looking after each other, sharing what they know, and in other ways helping each other. Stephanie remarks, "I could not possibly count all the times I arrived at my desk to find a lesson plan or offers to help me." She adds, "I think the main way new teachers learn is much more informal, through interactions with other teachers. I learned so much just from watching other teachers in the Social Studies office interact with each other and with their students. By observing other teachers, I was able to see what works for them and see how I can adapt what they do to use in my own classroom" (Stephanie Neuberger, personal communication, June 2003).

This informal coming together of teachers in a community of practice is a powerful way to improve teaching and learning. As important as formal mentoring programs are and as hard as Eric, the department director, works to encourage colleagues, to enable learning, and to ensure that Stevenson's vision and values are respected and supported, without the development of voluntary and informal communities of practice, Stevenson (like other schools) runs the risk of promoting contrived collegiality rather than the real thing. Andy Hargreaves (1994) views contrived collegiality as character-ized by a set of formal, specific procedures to increase the attention being given to joint teacher planning and consultation. It can be seen in initiatives such as peer coaching, mentor teaching, joint planning in specially provided rooms, formally scheduled meetings, and clear job descriptions and training programs for those in con-sultative roles. Contrived collegiality has merit when administra-tors design those initiatives to get collegiality going in schools where little has existed before.

By the same token Eric, the other directors, the principal, and other members of Stevenson's formal leadership team are obliged by their roles to take the lead in ensuring that Stevenson's purposes and values are represented and are used as a basis for making deci-sions. They are the promoters and protectors of Stevenson's collab-orative culture. Key to their efforts is the belief that learning to-gether in community lays the foundation for creating a success-ful school. They seek to help schools get smarter, knowing that smarter schools help students get smarter. We often have to start with contrived collegiality orchestrated by the school's formal lead-ership. But for a true collaborative culture to emerge, contrived col-legiality must become real—and real depends on the communities of practice that teachers create.

Communities of practice bubble up as a result of felt needs of teachers to cooperate. Collaborative cultures are more deliberate, having been initiated and supported by leaders from above. They differ from communities of practice in that they become institu-tionalized as part of the formal norm system of the school and as part of its organizational structure. Ideally the two come together as one, creating a strong bond of people committed to working together toward goals and purposes that they share.

In Stephanie's case Laura and Laurie and other teachers stepped forward to extend an invitation to join them in a special partnership that resembled a shared practice. Friendship, relational trust, a commitment to help each other, to learn together, to be part of a shared practice are hallmarks of a community of practice. Eric values this sense of community, but his responsibility is to put together a collaborative team that commits itself to embodying Stevenson's culture and that aggregates its competence in order to be more able to improve student learning.

In a sense communities of practice serve individual needs and intents. Institutionalized collaborative cultures build on the personal strengths of individuals and transfer this improved individual capacity into aggregated organizational competence that serves the school's goals. Richard Elmore (2002) refers to benefits that serve individual interests and that build their capacity on their own terms as a private good. By contrast, aggregated organizational competence that serves school purposes is a public good. Together they create a powerful force of capacity and commitment that helps develop more effective pathways to student learning.

In sum, successful collaborative cultures are formally recognized communities of practice that work deeply and firmly to bring people together around themes of practice. They state their purposes publicly, review the commitments that they make to embody the norms and purposes in their practice, and they create an environment of accountability that is informal but public. What purposes do we share? How can we best work together to achieve them? How well are we doing? These are centerpiece questions in both formal and informal conversations. This bubbling up and trickling down suggests that we might think of leadership as "binary" (Evans, 1996). Binary leadership is a source of energy that emerges from the obligations and commitment that define teacher and administrator reciprocal role relationships.

Evans believes that principals and other designated leaders are essential to schools' working well. In his experience with successful schools

> There is always a powerful principal, someone with passion and presence (that is, someone with conviction and confidence, not necessarily flamboyance), someone who seems competent enough to make *any* system of governance work. In most cases, this principal was one of the co-creators of the school's shared-decision-making and collaborative efforts. Some are more charismatic than others, some are better organized, some hold more firmly a "first among equals" status. But I have never known, and cannot imagine, a school in which empowerment and participation flourish over time without a strong principal [1996, p. 242].

Thus leadership that bubbles up and leadership that trickles down are both critical. While one or the other might work for a while, strong leadership that brings about sustained success over time needs both. But, whatever its source, this leadership must be based on ideas and must be based on the principle of entitlement. No one has an automatic right to lead. Leadership, be it bubbling up or trickling down, is always based on some source of authority. Sometimes this authority comes from one's role and the obligations and the responsibilities it entails. And sometimes this authority comes from one's ability to help others achieve their purposes.

Dan Galloway, Stevenson's principal, takes his roles as steward of the school's purposes and values and as capacity builder seriously. His goal is to build the aggregated organizational competence needed for Stevenson to achieve its goals and purposes:

> At the beginning of the school year, once our goals, projects, and initiatives have been identified, I meet with each instructional area director to collaboratively

develop their departmental goals, projects, and initiatives. I ensure that each department has goals that are tied to helping achieve the district goals. For example, one of our school's (and districts') goals is to ensure that 100 percent of our graduates meet or exceed expectations on the state testing. So, when I meet with each director, goals are identified for their department that will assist in accomplishing that goal.

At Stevenson High School, we are committed to building the leadership capacity of our staff and we believe in dispersing the leadership throughout the organization. Our administrative structure is less hierarchical and more flat, which means that many people share in the responsibility of providing leadership in our school. Our focus is on collaboration, not line of authority. We have defined our mission and we know the type of school we want to be. We have developed shared commitments that guide our behaviors to ensure that our daily work moves us toward realizing our vision. We consider ourselves to be a professional learning community. As principal, I am a steward of that vision and work to ensure that our daily activities are grounded in it [Dan Galloway, personal communication, June 2003].

Galloway asks nothing of others that he would not ask from himself. As steward his leadership is consistently based on ideas rather than personality.

Division directors play key roles at Stevenson and much of its success can be attributed to them. John Carter, director of the Math Division, echoes Galloway's sentiments about the importance of stewardship and sees himself as both a capacity builder and a protector:

As a capacity builder my role goes far beyond the traditional role of professional developer. My goal is to help each teacher learn to make decisions about teaching, curriculum, content, and interpersonal relationships, using sound evidence and multiple perspectives. I structure our designated staff development time to provide teachers with the opportunity to continue to grow in content knowledge and pedagogical content knowledge. Through the various team interactions, I provide teachers with the experiences and feedback needed to grow into fully collaborative partners in the division. Our focus is to always approach topics from a data-gathering point of view so that we can make decisions and proceed using the data to support us.

As a protector I have to protect the department vision and assure progress toward it. I need to be able to base decisions and priorities on the direction we have set for ourselves—and occasionally remind people of it. Listening well to individuals as they express their opinions and feelings is an important part of balancing the progress and the collective emotional health of the division. While learning can be difficult it need not be overwhelming [John Carter, personal communication, June 2003].

Some Principles for Organizing

The Stevenson experience suggests that to get both smarter schools and smarter students, leaders everywhere in a school need to pay attention to four principles for organizing:

- *The Principle of Cooperation.* When teachers cooperate with each other by working together, trying out ideas together, examining student work together, and helping each other, teaching and learning are enhanced. Further, cooperation helps overcome the effects of isolation that too often characterize teaching. In collaborative cultures organizational structures enhance cooperation among teachers.

- *The Principle of Empowerment.* Empowering teachers contributes to ownership, increased commitment, and increased motivation to work. When teachers feel like pawns rather than players who can control their own behavior, they are likely to respond with reduced commitment, mechanical behavior, indifference, and even dissatisfaction and alienation. Collaborative cultures are designed to enhance empowerment among teachers. But empowerment does not leave teachers or anyone else free to do whatever they please. Empowerment refers to obligation, duty, and accountability. Thus the empowerment rule that collaborative cultures follow is this: People are free to do what they wish providing that what they do embodies the school's shared values and commitments.

- *The Principle of Responsibility.* Most teachers want more responsibility. Responsibility enhances the importance and significance of their work and provides a tangible basis for recognizing their success. In collaborative cultures designated leaders and organizational structures encourage teachers to accept a fair share of responsibility for the school's achieving its purposes. Principals know that discretion for teachers is necessary for this responsibility to be accepted and authentic.

- *The Principle of Accountability.* Accountability is related to empowerment and responsibility. It is not likely that someone is empowered or has real responsibility unless that person is also accountable. Accountability provides a healthy measure of excitement, challenge, and importance that raises the stakes just enough so that achievement means something. In collaborative cultures goals and purposes are public and the ways in which people achieve them are public too, as are the outcomes. The public nature of what is going on and the reflection and inquiry that accompanies what the school is doing provides a continuous stream of accountability that is both formative and summative.

Connections

Connections are important in building collaborative cultures.[2] For these cultures to work we have to be connected somehow, somewhere. Being connected to the school and to our colleagues is a way to become connected to ourselves, to know that we belong, to know that we count for something, and most important to know that we are valued.

But not all connections count the same way. Not all connections, for example, are community oriented. Some connections are *rational* and other connections are *cultural*. Rational connections are based primarily on the pursuit of self-interest and involve trades. When we choose rational connections, it is assumed that motivation results from logically weighing options and selecting the one that gives us the most benefits at the least cost. This sort of exchange is clearly understood in the corporate world. Employers agree to provide their employees with certain economic benefits and other amenities. In return employees agree to follow job rules and to meet job expectations. Similar bargains are struck in other sectors of our formal society.

Cultural connections, by contrast, are more covenantal than contractual. They are bargains of the heart and soul. They are based primarily on loyalties, purposes, and sentiments that emerge from stated and unstated understandings and commitments that obligate people to each other and that obligate people to the school. Covenants are much more than agreements. They are promises.

[2] This discussion of connections and opportunities and capacity is drawn from Sergiovanni, 2001, pp. 63–65, 109–110.

Promises play an important role in the functioning of collaborative cultures. They imply certain mutually held actions and commitments that are considered obligatory. Unlike legal documents and other formal agreements that spell out all the technical details, covenants are planted within the hearts of people, bind them together morally, and obligate them morally to the conditions of the covenant. Cultural connections and covenantal relationships are the foundational pillars of collaborative cultures that function as communities of responsibility. Cultural connections and covenantal relationships are the sources of authority for Carter's and Galloway's leadership at Stevenson. Without these connections it would not be possible for these leaders to be successful stewards devoted to protecting Stevenson's value system and devoted to building the capacities of teachers who are responsible for embodying those ideas.

Hallmarks of a Learning Community

At the point where communities of practice bubble up and collaborative cultures trickle down, learning communities emerge. Learning communities are good at *maximizing* their learning. They learn from both successes and failures. They are good at *continuous learning* and at *dispersing* what they know, especially to places where it is most needed. Learning communities have faith in the *craft knowledge* and wisdom of those closest to the classroom. They are on constant lookout for new learning opportunities as ways to *expand* what they know and can do. They believe in *collaboration* and view learning as a *professional obligation*. How does your school measure up to these hallmarks? Use the inventory in Exhibit 6.1 to find out.[3] Be sure to provide examples. Share your perceptions with a colleague.

[3] For a similar list see Mintzberg, Ahlstrand, and Lampel, 1998, pp. 214–215.

Exhibit 6.1. Inventory: Hallmarks of a Learning Community

How true are the following statements in your department, grade level, team, or school?

1. The Principle of Maximization: We learn as much from our failures as we do from our successes.

    Never   Sometimes   Always
     1   2   3   4   5

Give examples _____

2. The Principle of Continuous Learning: We don't wait for a time to learn but are continuously learning. For us learning is an ongoing process and not an event.

    Never   Sometimes   Always
     1   2   3   4   5

Give examples _____

3. The Principle of Dispersion: We share what we learn with others. We see to it that knowledge finds its way to the teachers or units that need it the most.

    Never   Sometimes   Always
     1   2   3   4   5

Give examples _____

4. The Principle of Craft Knowledge: Designated leaders assume that those of us who are closest to the classroom and its work are often in the best position to know about teaching and learning. Competence is an important entitlement to leadership regardless of one's position in the school. And craft knowledge plays a key role in building competence.

    Never   Sometimes   Always
     1   2   3   4   5

Give examples _____

5. The Principle of Expansion: We are on the watch for what we can learn and use from those outside our unit or school. We pay particular attention to all we can learn from other schools and from outside experts.

   Never   Sometimes   Always

   1   2   3   4   5

   Give examples _____

6. The Principle of Collaboration: We take every opportunity to collaborate with each other.

   Never   Sometimes   Always

   1   2   3   4   5

   Give examples _____

7. The Principle of Professionalism: We believe that continuous learning is a professional virtue. We believe that we are obligated to embody this virtue in our practice.

   Never   Sometimes   Always

   1   2   3   4   5

   Give examples _____

Some Findings

Opportunity and capacity can help make teacher learning and the use of collaborative cultures a natural part of a school's life. As a result of her research, Kanter (1997) found that opportunity and capacity were essential for effective performance. In schools, *opportunity* refers to the perception that teachers have of their options for increasing knowledge, skills, and rewards. Do teachers have the opportunity to learn, to figure out ways in which challenging standards can be met? Do teachers have the opportunity to respond to the needs of their students? Do teachers have the opportunity to respond to increases in responsibility and increases in the challenges that they face?

Capacity refers to the ability to get things done, to gather the resources that one needs in order to get things done, and to interact with others who can help get things done. Kanter warns that when opportunity and capacity are diminished, interest and excitement in work decreases. McLaughlin and Yee (1988) found that enhanced levels of opportunity and capacity resulted in teachers' experiencing greater stimulation at work and higher levels of motivation. They found that teachers' effectiveness was directly related to the opportunities that teachers had to develop basic competence, to experience challenge in teaching, to receive feedback about their importance, to get support for trying new ideas, and to get support for their own growth. McLaughlin and Yee suggest that there is much that leaders can do to directly improve opportunities for learning. But as working together becomes even more important in schools and as the learning curves that will be needed become more demanding, leaders will have to focus less and less on providing direct leadership and more and more on building substitutes for leadership into the very structure and culture of schooling itself. Substitutes for leadership are the pathways and norms leaders build that allow, encourage, and enhance teacher learning and teacher collaboration. "While the leader must learn too, and sometimes can be the main learner, more commonly it is a collective system that learns" (Mintzberg, Ahlstrand, and Lampel, 1998, p. 208). *Collaborative cultures mean collective brain power* should become our motto.

As part of their study of the characteristics and effectiveness of collaborative cultures in the Chicago city schools, Sebring and her colleagues (1995) examined the extent to which high-achieving and low-achieving schools were developing a shared focus and shared responsibility for learning. They found that while teachers' talking to each other about their work (reflective dialog), having the opportunity to involve themselves in peer coaching and in the sharing of teaching methods (deprivatization), and developing expectations about what students should learn (shared norms) were important, these variables did not discriminate between low-achieving and high-achieving schools. Both groups of schools reported similar amounts of these characteristics. Apparently while these characteristics may be necessary for collaborative cultures to emerge and strengthen, they are not sufficient to bring about high levels of student achievement.

Two other characteristics of collaborative cultures, however, did affect student achievement. They were "peer collaboration" and "focus on student learning":

> Almost 75 percent of the low-achieving elementary schools are below the systemwide median on the collaboration measure. The typical teacher in a low-achieving school indicates that she does not coordinate instruction with other grades or collaborate with colleagues to make the school run effectively. Similarly, about a quarter of the teachers in low-achieving schools disagree with all of the items that compose the focus on student learning scale: "This school sets high standards for academic performance"; "This school has well defined learning expectations"; and "When making important decisions, this school always focuses on what is best for student learning" (Sebring, and others, 1996, p. 70).

A key factor that weaves together all of the five indicators of collaborative cultures identified in the Chicago study is the extent to which faculty feel a "collective responsibility" for the success of the school. When levels of collegiality are high, when teachers behave like members of a community of practice, when teachers feel morally obligated to meet their commitments to each other and to the school's purposes, and when teachers are committed to working together to do what is best for students, collective responsibility is high. Collective responsibility is a quality much more abundant in high-achieving schools than in low-achieving schools (p. 71).

As a result of their research on collaborative cultures, Druskat and Wolff (2001) identified three conditions that are essential for team success:

- A sense of trust among members
- A sense of group identity
- A sense of group efficacy

Without any one of the three, team members are more likely to go through the motions of cooperation but will not be fully engaged. "To be most effective, the team needs to create emotionally intelligent norms—the attitudes and behaviors that eventually become habits—that support behaviors for building trust, group identity, and group efficacy" (p. 82).

According to Druskat and Wolff (2001), numerous studies demonstrate that teams become more creative and more productive as they are able to achieve higher levels of participation, cooperation, and collaboration among members. Collaboration increases the amount of collective brainpower available to share with others and to help solve problems. And you need mutual trust among team members, a sense of identity as a group with unique character and personality, and beliefs that collaboration is usually more effective than working alone. The result is better decisions, more creative solutions, and higher levels of performance.

Each of these factors helps to build norm systems in schools or to re-norm existing systems. Since teachers, administrators, and students alike are norm referenced, much of their behavior becomes predictable as norms are established. The right norms provide the insurance policy that leaders need to make sure that collaborative cultures have wide discretion within a framework of agreed-upon expectations and commitments. The idea of collaborative cultures is inherently an idea of empowerment. Together, capacity and commitment help each member of the culture to be more powerful and to have a heightened sense of efficacy. But, as suggested in the

Principle of Empowerment, when empowerment is offered the first question to be asked is, Empowered to do what? Everyone plays by the same rule: You are free to do what you think is best providing that what you do embodies the values, ideas, promises, and commitments that we share as a school. It is this view of empowerment that strengthens the heartbeat of a school.

It seems reasonable to accept the idea that norms that build trust, identity, and efficacy are key to effective collaborative cultures. But how do these powerful norms come about? Druskat and Wolff note, "In our research, we saw them being introduced from any of five basic directions: by formal team leaders, by informal team leaders, by courageous followers, through training, or by the larger organizational culture" (2001, p. 89). By definition leadership and norms go together. Thus the effectiveness of leadership is measured by its impact on cultural norms. And since leadership bubbles up from below and trickles down from above, there is no clear-cut monopoly on involvement in norm setting. In an environment of leadership by entitlement, if you care enough about the school and its work and if you care enough for your colleagues, then you are obliged to be concerned about what the existing norms are and whether these norms are helpful in achieving our purposes.

Veteran Stevenson teacher Carol Levin's comments provide a fitting summary to the story of collaborative cultures and how they can work to build the capacity of teachers and to make schools more effective places for students to learn.

> At a school like Stevenson where collaboration is the norm, it's difficult to imagine any other kind of working and learning environment. Some might suspect that collaboration would intensify competition. In fact, the opposite is true. In individual sports, each player struggles to stand out above the rest, but players win by contributing and pulling for the entire team. Collaboration is a team sport and it works.

On a small scale, collaboration is what happens every day among colleagues in department offices as we refine our daily lesson plans. We talk as a matter of course about student comprehension, student skills, teacher effectiveness, and how to improve on them all. On a larger continuum, the collaborative culture at Stevenson manifests itself in team meetings that actively involve every teacher in the building. Teaching teams consistently come together reinforced by their common subject matter and their unflagging efforts to push both the curriculum and student success forward.

The team approach is successful because teachers feel we are given the *opportunity* to meet productively, not be robotically brought together for some forced reason. Teachers work comfortably together because we are empowered to generate goals from within our own ranks, goals that are important to our instruction, goals that we perceive as beneficial to the team and to our students. Because teams monitor their own progress, it's very easy to keep setting goals that "raise the bar." The collaborative configuration encourages both individual and collective dialogue and reflection. Teachers share "best practices," successful approaches, failures—which sometimes teach more than successes—and new ideas. We feel that our voices are regularly solicited, considered, and valued by our colleagues. No wonder we "buy into" collaboration [Carol Levin, personal communication, June 2003].

7

Using Ideas to Back Up Leadership

Idea-based leadership provides a more powerful foundation for leadership in a school than does mandated leadership, leadership based on position, or leadership based on personality. All four have legitimate roles to play, but it is ideas that belong at the center. Ideas back up our leadership by providing a source of authority for what we do—a source of authority with moral overtones.

This chapter provides examples of ideas at work and discusses eight basic competencies that leaders will need to use ideas effectively. Ideas have the greatest impact when they are woven into stories. Howard Gardner (1995) believes that the ultimate impact of leadership depends on the stories the leader communicates to others. Sometimes the story line emerges as the result of conversations with teachers and conversations with others and then is adopted by the leader, who acts as a spokesperson. At other times the story line is a poignant description of a series of events that happened in a school—events that others resonate with and find meaning in. Story lines, for example, might be themed to caring, every student can learn given the right conditions, teacher learning is key to the school's success, parents are essential partners in teaching and learning, and organizational character of a school is critical to its success. If the leader is effective, then these stories become the school's stories, providing the sense of identity and coherence that holds things together as the school struggles to make its stories a reality. School stories become part of the school's idea structure and make it possible for administrators and others to lead with ideas.

Choosing a Strategy for Leading and Doing

Everyone agrees that improving the academic, developmental, and civic lives of teachers and children in schools is an important purpose. There is, however, disagreement about how this goal is to be achieved. Whatever else leadership is, it involves choosing from among several strategies to achieve purposes. What options do we have when choosing a strategy? One is to use mandates that specify minimum standards, expectations, and rules in detail and provide the management systems necessary to ensure that schools will comply with these mandates (McDonnell and Elmore, 1987). Mandates are accompanied by close monitoring and typically include penalties for noncompliance. A related option is to rely on incentives that trade rewards for compliance. Mandates and incentives come up short because they create uniformity, reduce variation, stifle creativity, focus attention on minimums, lead to calculated involvement, and encourage the maximization of self-interest at the expense of the common good. They lack the ability to produce future value for students and their parents.

Two alternative strategies that can help provide the leadership we need are learning together (capacity building) and involving people early in the process of decision making as a way to build trust and credibility (grassroots democratic participation). Both of these strategies are able to produce future value on a continuous basis. Both expand value as demand expands, change value as expectations change, and create new value as new requirements for learning emerge. But there's no need to choose sides. It is not one strategy versus another but rather which strategy will be emphasized more and which will be emphasized less.

Capacity building, for example, creates intellectual capital by emphasizing the development of knowledge, competence, and skill of parents, teachers, and others who have a stake in the local school community. As parents and other citizens develop the ability to provide the support that students need to belong and to be successful at school, they get smarter. And smarter parents mean smarter students. But intellectual capital is more than what we know as individuals and more than what one group knows collectively. Intellectual material not only has to be developed and captured, it has to be formalized and put to work on behalf of school purposes if higher-value assets are to be produced for students and teachers. "Intelligence becomes an asset when some useful order is created out of free-floating brainpower—that is, when it is given coherent form . . .; when it is captured in a way that allows it to be described, shared, and exploited; and when it can be deployed to do something that could not be done if it remained scattered around like so many coins in a gutter. Intellectual capital is packaged useful knowledge" (Stewart, 1997, p. 67). Leadership for learning, therefore, is not just about developing and gathering what people know but packaging it into frameworks that are useful in enhancing school practice.

This view of leadership is the theory behind Stevenson High School's building of collaborative cultures and its emphasis on communities of practice that bring team members together into a shared practice. This view of leadership is the theory behind taking a trust-first perspective on vision. Trust, for example, helps with the change process and helps make turning visions into reality easier. This view of leadership is the theory for using shared action statements that represent the commitment of various school constituents—commitments that provide people with road maps on one hand and moral obligations to keep their word on the other. And since packaged information is useful only when strategies become action, this is the theory for emphasizing the operational requirements, the nitty-gritty planning, and the doing that results in things getting done.

We still have to go further because knowing what to do and how to do it is not enough. Local capacity needs to be put to work to actually improve schools. This is where involving people at the grassroots comes in. By emphasizing such involvement locals learn more, experience more sense and meaning, and build community connections. These are examples of social capital needed to support high levels of authentic leadership and learning in schools.

In sum, an idea structure typically includes a school's bank of strategies that get worked out and saved over time. As Mintzberg, Ahlstrand, and Lampel (1998) suggest, strategies appear first as patterns from the past, then as plans for the future, and finally as perspectives to guide overall behavior. Thus we can think of strategy as

- A plan for our intended purposes

- A pattern of how we functioned in the past

- A niche or trademark that gives us a unique identity

- Our theory of action, our predictable ways of doing things over time

- Our tactics—our decisions at any given moment in time

Effective strategy making is a process of learning over time. "While the leader must learn too, and sometimes can be the main learner, more commonly it is the collective system that learns: there are many potential strategists in most organizations" (Mintzberg, Ahlstrand, and Lampel, 1998, p. 208). To Mintzberg and his colleagues the role of leadership serves less to create strategies and more to manage the process of strategic learning. This leading and learning enables responsive and effective strategies to emerge. Intelligence becomes packaged and useful information when schools get the "strategy thing" right.

Competencies for Leadership

By emphasizing learning and by emphasizing the involvement of people in making important decisions about what needs to be done and how, leaders focus less on managerial and motivational roles and more on developer and community-building roles. To be successful as developers and community builders, leaders will need to back up their leadership with ideas. And for this approach to be successful, leaders will have to master eight basic competencies: the management of attention, the management of meaning, the management of trust, and the management of self (Bennis, 1989), as well as the management of paradox, the management of effectiveness, the management of follow-up, and the management of responsibility.[1]

The management of *attention* is the ability to focus others on values, ideas, goals, and purposes that bring people together and that provide a rationale, a source of authority for what goes on in the school. Leaders manage attention by what they say, what they reward, how they spend time, the behaviors they emphasize, and the reasons they give for the decisions they make. They practice *purposing*, defined as that continuous stream of action that induces clarity, consensus, and commitment regarding schools purposes (Vaill, 1984).

Purposing involves both the vision of the leader and the covenant that the school shares. In successful schools consensus runs deep. It is not enough to have worked out what people in the school stand for and what they expect to accomplish. Leaders continuously struggle to develop a binding and solid agreement that represents a value system for living together and forms the basis for decisions and actions (Sergiovanni, 1992).

The management of *meaning* is the ability to connect teachers, parents, and students to the school in such a way that they find their lives useful, sensible, and valued. Even the mundane routines of schools are valued and are connected to the larger purposes and meanings that define who people are, why they are in the school, why the school needs them, and why their participation with the school is worthwhile. Together the management of attention and the management of meaning answer these questions: What are our

[1] This discussion of the eight basic competencies is drawn in part from Sergiovanni, 2001, pp. 47–54, and from Sergiovanni, 2003, pp. 17-21.

priorities? What are our commitments to each other? Why are they important? How do they link to the ordinary things that we do? These messages help people become connected to each other and to the school, building hope and commitment and raising levels of civility and academic engagement.

The management of *trust* is the ability to be viewed as credible, legitimate, and honest. Bennis (1989) uses the term "constancy" (p. 21) to communicate that whether parents, teachers, and students like what a leader does or not, they always know where that leader is coming from, what that leader stands for, and why that leader is doing things. It is not enough to make decisions; leaders have to explain them and show how they are linked to the heartbeat of the school as well.

But trust, as pointed out in earlier chapters, has more than personal qualities. It is a key ingredient in the development of social capital. Coleman (1988) found that social capital correlates with the development of human capital (more learning in a school, for example), a finding confirmed by Putnam (2000) and more recently by Bryk and Schneider (2002). These latter researchers provide a compelling case for strong links between the amount of "relational trust" found in a school and made available to students and the students' subsequent academic performance. Not only does social capital seem related to learning, it is also a social need of students and others. If social capital is not available to students, they create it for themselves by turning more and more to the student subculture and its norms. Too often, however, student norms stand in the way of student achievement.

The management of *self* is the ability to know who you are, what you believe, and why you do the things you do. When a leader's behavior can be defended in such a way that others at least understand and at least respect that behavior, then self-knowledge has been achieved. Despite the importance of the management of self, too often this competency is neglected. The management of self is an art worth developing—but one not easily achieved without a measure of practical intelligence. Practical intelligence is the ability to know how things work and the ability to make things work. The cultivation of keen insight into human nature and the putting together of this knowledge in some useful way are examples (Sternberg, 1996).

The management of *paradox* is the ability to bring together ideas that seem to be at odds with each other. Combining an emphasis on rigorous standards with a refusal to impose standardization or compromise local discretion; expecting a great deal from teachers while empowering them to take control of their professional lives; responding to adolescent needs for independence while providing the disciplined safe havens they need; involving parents without compromising professional autonomy; and bringing everyone together in a common quest united by shared values while honoring diversity and promoting innovative ideas are examples. When implemented, these seemingly contradictory ideas can actually bring us together, make us brighter and stronger, and help us achieve larger purposes. The management of paradox is easier when leaders look to ideas, values, and visions of the common good as a moral sense of authority for what they do.

The management of *effectiveness* is the ability to focus on the development of capacity in a school that allows it to improve performance over time. Key to the management of effectiveness is how school success is understood and measured. When effectiveness is managed well, school success involves getting results and more. School success also involves learning and cultivating relationships. Learning builds the capacity of teachers to know more about their work, to figure out how to create better pathways to success, and to improve practice as a result. Relationships, as pointed out earlier, provide the support that teachers need to come together as a community of learners and a community of practice. Thus, determining the success of any initiative requires answers to three sets of questions:

- What is being accomplished? Are the results of high quality? Does what is being done make sense to parents and other constituencies?

- What are they learning about their work? Are they
  likely to be more effective the next time around as a
  result? How are they sharing what they are learning?

- Is everyone working together as a community of practice? Is everyone supporting each other and helping
  each other? Is the community proud of what they are
  doing and do they enjoy working together?

Trust first and then vision. Next comes strategy followed by
action plans. But success requires that we go to the next step.
Strategies and action plans need day-to-day planning and day-to-
day execution. Who will do what, by when, and with whom? What
specific training will be needed that will enable us to be successful?
A system of supervision needs to be in place to monitor what is
going on and to provide in-class and on-call professional development. If teachers need help, for example, they ought to be able to
get it on the spot—when they need it. Other questions to ask: What
kinds of assessments will be needed? Who will be responsible for all
the little day-by-day things that need to be done for our action plans
to become realities? Leaders, in other words, need to be competent
in the management of *follow-up*.

Too often leaders seem to tire when it gets down to details, pre-
ferring to delegate these responsibilities to others. But without
follow-up by the full complement of a school's leadership and the
full complement of a school district's leadership the job rarely gets
done to standard. Execution of plans takes detailed, careful, and
continuous supervision, support, and assessment. Pretty or not, these
details are needed to move the ball across the goal line. No matter
how brilliant the game plan and how exciting the game itself, if you
can't get across the goal line you will not get your plans implemented. Larry Bossidy ("What Does the Swing . . .," 2003) points
out that strategic plans are both brilliant and ignored. Once the
brilliance plays itself out and the hard work begins, superintendents

and other top leaders too often move on to other issues and develop newer and even more brilliant strategic plans. In this environment, the original plans rarely have a chance to take root, to become institutionalized as operational policy.

Sometimes the problem is superintendent turnover or turnover of other key leaders. New superintendents arrive and visions are renewed. New strategic plans are crafted, and after three or four years when the real work of implementation needs to be done, the superintendent moves on, often repeating the pattern elsewhere. And a superintendent who stays is likely to delegate responsibility for managing the implementation process to others so as to be able to give attention to "more pressing" problems. Despite the glamour inherent in this kind of strategic planning and the illusions of change that accompany this planning, very little really happens for long in the school. In short, successful implementation takes follow-up. Included in this follow-up is detailed, careful, and continuous supervision that emphasizes learning, and this is accompanied by assessment.

The management of follow-up is more likely to be accomplished when superintendents and other high officials are involved in the day-to-day struggle of implementation. Top leadership, for example, should participate in professional development training. Learning walks or walkthroughs should become a part of their weekly routine as they visit schools and classrooms to examine firsthand what is going on and what progress is being made. Responsibility for follow-up can be shared but not delegated. Unless leaders are in the midst of the implementation process and unless they play key roles in its management and assessment, implementation of any quality and for any length of time is likely to evaporate. Teacher leadership, too, is critical to successful follow-up. Without teacher leadership we change how things look but not how things work.

The management of *responsibility* involves the internalization of values and purposes that obligate people to meet their commitments to each other and to the school. Professionals have long known the power of extrinsic rewards and the power of intrinsic rewards in motivating people. As suggested in the Introduction, extrinsic and intrinsic rewards comprise two widely accepted motivational rules: *what is rewarded gets done* and *what is rewarding gets done*. But in reality people are motivated by three motivational rules, with the third being *what one feels a duty or obligation to do, gets done*. When people feel obligated to do something not only do they do it well but they do it even when the going gets tough. They do it whether it is pleasant or not and whether they want to or not. This third motivational rule is important because duty and obligation are not only stronger than gain or pleasure, they sustain themselves over time.

Thus the best way to manage responsibility is to evoke duty and obligation as motivators. This is done when schools are helped to become not just learning and caring communities but communities of responsibility. As suggested earlier, in communities of responsibility leadership is based on a different kind of authority—one embedded in the ideas that encourage us to respond from within, to become self-managing. Instead of following the leader, the emphasis is on following commitments, promises, obligations, validated research, sound principles, agreed-upon standards, and other ideas. In communities of responsibility it is norms, values, beliefs, purposes, goals, standards, hopes, and dreams that provide the ideas for morally based leadership. These ideas are not mandated scripts that require carbon-copy conformity. They are instead more like frameworks that provide people with a heightened sense of understanding, meaning, and significance. When leadership is morally based, its effect on spirit, commitment, and results is not only strong but obligatory, allowing the school to function with commitment and determination.

In sum, the eight basic competencies are the basis for developing and using an idea-based leadership. This use changes the sources of authority for leadership from bureaucratic requirements and from the leader's personal charm quotient to purposes, values, theories, and other cognitive frameworks. Though bureaucratic and personal requirements may be helpful, they should not be placed at the center in deciding what to do. Richard Elmore (2003) sums up the importance of substance in leadership to school improvement as follows:

> The U.S. fetish for leadership leads to an overemphasis on the personal attributes of school leaders and a correspondingly weak focus on the technical, cognitive demands of instructional practice and the affective and behavioral responses of those demands. Successful leaders have an explicit theory of what good instructional practice looks like. They model their own learning and theories of learning in their work, work publicly on the improvement of their own practice, and engage others in powerful discourse about good instruction. These leaders understand that improving school performance requires transforming a fundamentally weak instructional core, and the culture that surrounds it, into a strong, explicit body of knowledge about powerful teaching and learning that is accessible to those who are willing to learn it [p. 10].

Ineffective leadership process is trumped by substance.

Some Examples

Every leader has to address the issue of choosing the basis for deciding what will be done and how progress will be assessed. To Stevenson High School the basis is such ideas as the collective commitments that constituent groups promise to meet in order for their work to better embody the school's vision. And it is the use of collaborative cultures that connects faculty to each other and provides the norms for working together on student academic and developmental needs.

For Gompers Elementary School the basis is the Articles of Faith to which members of the school community adhere. The hope that the Gompers faculty has for student success is based on faith in the

Comer process and faith in the importance of teaching to the whole child if students are to succeed. It seems old-fashioned to worry about the whole child these days when increasingly, academic matters no longer support developmental matters but replace them. This whole, the Gompers faculty feels, is greater than the sum of its parts and all of the parts are needed to be successful academically. In both cases ideas are used to back up leadership.

The Principles of Learning

Many schools adopt theories of action, usually in the form of assumptions presumed to be true, to back up leadership. Sometimes these assumptions are based on convictions, but usually they are research based too. Perhaps the best known research-based theory of action these days is the Principles of Learning developed by the Institute for Learning at the University of Pittsburgh. The principles are summarized in Exhibit 7.1. First tested in New York City's District 2, the principles have been refined and are now used as a source of authority for teaching and learning decisions in a number of urban school districts including Bridgeport, Pittsburgh, Providence, and San Diego. When linked to standards the Principles of Learning not only inform what will be taught, they govern how students will be taught and how they will be assessed. Yet there are no scripts. Plenty of room exists for teachers to use their ingenuity and to rely on pedagogical methods that they understand and enjoy.

Still, there are limits. A serious walkthrough of classrooms should reveal that the Principles of Learning are reflected in the pedagogical decisions that teachers make. In Resnick and Glennan's (2001) words: "These principles do not constitute a rigid specification of a design. Specifics of the organization and operations vary from one district to another, depending on a district's history, its size, the population it serves, and the particular characteristics of its staff. Not static, these principles evolve as the Institute and its member districts learn from their experiences" (p. 5).

Exhibit 7.1. Principles of Learning

Organizing for Effort

- A clear, high, minimum set of standards that every student is expected to meet is established in each subject.

- All students are taught a curriculum that prepares them to meet the standards.

- Additional instruction and learning time is provided for students who need it in order to meet the standards.

- When there are special learning opportunities, a willingness to do the work is the primary admission criterion.

- Students are responsible for completing academic work that has been specified and negotiated.

- There are specified bodies of work (e.g., reading a certain number of books, writing a research paper, performing school service) that students must accomplish by the end of key stages of schooling.

Clear Expectations

- Standards that include models of student work are available to and discussed with students.

- Students judge their work with respect to the standards.

- Intermediate expectations leading to the formally measured standards are specified.

- Families and community are informed about the accomplishment standards that children are expected to achieve.

Fair and Credible Evaluations

- Exams and tests are referenced to standards and designed to be studied for. The exams and tests are valid when students directly prepare to take them.

Exhibit 7.1. Principles of Learning *(continued)*

- Exams, tests, and classwork are graded against absolute standards, not on a curve.

- A reporting system exists that makes it clear to students and their parents how they are progressing toward expected standards.

- Assessments validly test the full range of adopted standards.

- Curriculum and assessments are aligned.

- "Public accountability" assessment instruments and "instructional assessments" are aligned.

Recognition of Accomplishment

- Frequent and regular occasions for recognizing student accomplishment linked to standards are established.

- Recognitions mark real accomplishment—meeting a standard or intermediate expectations.

- Enough clearly demarcated progress points are set so that all students experience recognition and celebration of their accomplishments periodically.

- Families and other community members who matter to students participate in celebrations and recognition events.

- Employers and colleges recognize and ask for evidence of academic accomplishments for high school students.

Academic Rigor in a Thinking Curriculum

- Commitment to a Knowledge Core

    There is an articulated curriculum in each subject that avoids needless repetition and progressively deepens understanding of core concepts.

    The curriculum and instruction are clearly organized around major concepts specified in the standards.

    Teaching and assessment focus on students' mastery of core concepts.

Exhibit 7.1. Principles of Learning (*continued*)

- High-Thinking Demand

    In every subject, students are regularly expected to raise questions, to solve problems, to think, and to reason.

    Students are doing challenging, high-level assignments in every subject.

    Assignments in each subject include extended projects in which original work and revision to standards are expected.

    Students are challenged to construct explanations and to justify arguments in each subject.

    Instruction is organized to support reflection on learning processes and strategies.

- Active Use of Knowledge

    Each subject includes assignments that require students to synthesize several sources of information.

    Students in each subject are challenged to construct explanations and to test their understanding of concepts by applying and discussing them.

    Students' prior and out-of-school knowledge is used regularly in the teaching and learning process.

    Instructional tasks and classroom discourse require students to interpret texts and construct solutions.

Accountable Talk

- Engagement with Learning Through Talk

    A substantial portion of instructional time involves students in talk related to the concepts delineated in the standards.

    Accountable Talk sharpens students' thinking by reinforcing their ability to build and use knowledge.

    Teachers create the norms and skills of Accountable Talk in their classrooms by modeling appropriate forms of discussion and by questioning, probing, and leading conversations.

Exhibit 7.1. Principles of Learning *(continued)*

- Accountability to the Learning Community

  Students actively participate in classroom talk.

  Students listen attentively to one another.

  Students elaborate and build upon ideas and each others' contributions.

  Students work toward the goal of clarifying or expanding a proposition.

- Accountability to Knowledge

  Students make use of specific and accurate knowledge.

  Students provide evidence for claims and arguments.

  Students identify the knowledge that may not be available yet which is needed to address an issue.

- Accountability to Rigorous Thinking

  Students synthesize several sources of information.

  Students construct explanations.

  Students formulate conjectures and hypotheses.

  Students test their own understanding of concepts.

  Classroom talk is accountable to generally accepted standards of reasoning.

  Students challenge the quality of each other's evidence and reasoning.

  Classroom talk is accountable to standards of evidence appropriate to the subject matter.

Socializing Intelligence

- Beliefs

  I have the right and obligation to understand and make things work better.

  Problems yield to sustained effort.

Exhibit 7.1. Principles of Learning (*continued*)

- Skills

    Cognitive

    Social

- Disposition

    Habits of mind

    Tendency to try actively to analyze problems, ask questions, and get information

    Students acquire and use strategies for learning and problem solving.

    Students acquire and use strategies for appropriately getting and giving help in learning.

    Staff communicate to all students that they are already competent learners and are able to become even better through their persistent use of strategies and by reflecting on their efforts.

    Classroom practice holds students accountable for using learning, problem solving, and helping strategies.

    Students are persistent when working on challenging problems.

    Students regularly expect to do "better than before."

Self-Management of Learning

- Within the context of instruction and learning in the various subject areas, metacognitive strategies are explicitly modeled, identified, discussed, and practiced.

- Students are expected and taught to play an active role in monitoring and managing the quality of their learning.

- Teachers scaffold students' performance during initial stages of learning, then gradually remove supports.

Exhibit 7.1. Principles of Learning (*continued*)

Learning as Apprenticeship

- A substantial portion of instruction and learning occurs in the context of extended, interdisciplinary projects culminating in presentations of finished work.

- Student products meet publicly agreed upon standards of quality.

- Experts from within the school or from the community critique and guide student work.

- Learning strategies and thinking are overtly modeled and discussed.

Still, a fundamental assumption underlying the principles is that the details of teaching should not be left to teachers alone. Districts need to have an important say and in the name of instructional coherence should provide the same professional development and the same system of supervision and assessment for all teachers so that they will be successful in implementing the principles.

The bottom line is that instructional coherence should enhance but not undermine the work of teachers. Newmann, Smith, Allensworth, and Bryk (2001) clarify as follows:

> It is important to place strong instructional program coherence in perspective and to understand it not as the overriding task of school improvement or as a substitute for key supports for teaching and learning, but as a strategy for maximizing those supports. Strong instructional

program coherence could, for instance, undermine the development of teachers' professional community if it insisted on such regimented instruction that teachers had no opportunity to exercise expertise or raise questions about selected methods or programs. . . . Similarly, teachers' professional development opportunities might be made so uniform as to prevent individuals from learning skills unique to their teaching situation or background. The pursuit of greater program coherence must respond to appropriate forms of differentiation and be receptive to new or altered programming for staff and for students when clearly necessary. . . .

A school could become highly coherent (and could even increase student scores on standardized tests) by instituting instructional frameworks that are narrowly focused on the most rudimentary academic tasks. . . . Thus the ultimate value of strong program coherence will always depend on the perceived educational legitimacy of what students learn and how they learn it [p. 313].

It is fair to conclude from these caveats that despite the critical nature of instructional program coherence to the change process that addresses student learning, there really are limits. Instructional coherence works best when teachers are able to teach to their strengths. But teaching whatever they please whenever they please is not the answer to the problem. Think of coherence as a compass that carefully and deliberately points the way while allowing travelers enough discretion so that they may choose one path over another providing that instructional coherence is not endangered.

Lists of Five

It all comes back to stories. Whether brought in by the leader or percolating upward from the faculty and students, a school's stories communicate what is important and provide a way for teachers and others to gauge their fit with the school and its beliefs. As Howard Gardner explains,

> A leader is likely to achieve success only if she can construct and convincingly communicate a clear and persuasive story; appreciate the nature of the audience(s), including its changeable features; invest her own (or channel others') energy in the building and maintenance of an organization; embody in her own life the principal contours of the story; either provide direct leadership or find a way to achieve influence through indirect means; and, finally, find a way to understand and make use of, without being overwhelmed by, increasing technical expertise [1995, p. 302].

In a way ideas and the stories they communicate serve to persuade, to manage, to bind, and to legitimize. Ideas serve to persuade others, to convince them to adopt a point of view, and to feel obligated to embody these ideas and the story they represent in their practice. They serve as well to manage what is going on by providing public benchmarks that everyone can use to gauge the extent to which their own commitments and behaviors embody the ideas and the extent to which the school itself embodies these ideas. The development of lists of commitments by the various constituent groups at Adlai Stevenson High School presented in Chapter Three is an example. Teachers, administrators, students, and others examine their own work in light of its impact on the school's vision and identify ways in which their school lives can better embody the school's vision. How well are we doing? is always useful to ask. Various constituent groups can answer this question by examining their behaviors in light of the commitments that they make. Having made a public commitment, constituent groups feel obligated to embody these ideas in their practice, and thus the ideas themselves become accountability tools as well as guidelines for what people should or should not do.

Ideas serve also to bind people together. When ideas are shared, relationships among individuals who share these ideas change. They take on a moral character that provides tight and obligatory links among those who share the ideas. And finally, ideas serve to legitimize what it is that people do. Ideas thus serve as a source of authority for actions. No doubt teachers, principals, students, and other members of the school engage in their responsibilities for a variety of reasons themed to getting rewards or avoiding punishments. But the effectiveness of these strategies pales when compared to engaging in responsibilities because it is the right thing to do, or one feels obligated for other reasons. When push comes to shove, it is cognitive leadership that counts the most, not personality-based leadership and not bureaucratic leadership.

There is no mystery as to how to lead with ideas. The Principles of Learning offered by the Institute for Learning at the University of Pittsburgh, for example, provide a practical, documented, and formal list of lists whose source of authority is embedded in research and the experiences of those involved in school reform. Another, less formal, approach is for a school to decide to use its own promises and examples of commitments as part of its idea structure. These promises and commitments might be listed on posters that are scattered throughout the school—in classrooms, on corridor walls, in the cafeteria, the principal's office, the main foyer of the school, and in other public places. Different posters might address different themes:

- Five promises that we make to students

- Five promises that we make to each other

- Five characteristics that you will see in our teaching

- Five examples of great student work

- Five examples of great assignments that teachers give

- Five things that we expect from students

- Five things that we expect from parents

- Five things that parents can expect from us

- Five reasons why this is a great place to be a teacher

Engaging in conversations to reach agreement about promises, characteristics, examples, and expectations has value in and of itself. But when this work is made public, it provides both a set of guidelines for what it is that each of the role constituents ought to do and a set of ideas for holding each of the groups accountable. Of course some of these poster themes will be slow in changing. The five promises we make to students and the five promises we make to each other might be examples. The content of other poster themes, perhaps examples of great student work and examples of great assignments that teachers give, would be changed more frequently—perhaps once a month or once every two or three weeks. Providing lists of five is a compelling and easily understood way for a school to share and then evaluate its standards for what students ought to do and its standards for the kind of classroom environment that teachers ought to provide.

What about accountability? Think of the lists of five as public benchmarks that are widely shared. If teachers, administrators, parents, and students provide evidence that documents the extent to which they are keeping their promises, then we have in the works a meaningful and continuous accountability system with both formative and summative features.

The Power of Ideas

In a recent article syndicated by the Associated Press, Louise Chu (2003) reports that Coretta Scott King and other members of the Martin Luther King Jr. family are urging that a more effective strategy to bring about change is to rely less on Martin Luther King Jr. as a personality and more on the messages that he delivered. In the article Coretta Scott King is quoted as saying, "I think that what Martin would be happy with is that every person would follow his teachings and not depend on a leader." And further, "What he wanted to do was elevate the whole of humankind and [have] individuals understand that they can make a difference." King's eldest son, according to Chu, joins in urging people to focus less on personalities and more on ideas. "Men or women who are like Martin Luther King Jr. are rare. I don't believe we have the luxury to wait around until a Martin Luther King Jr. emerges." The message here is that too much is at stake to rely on charismatic or other forms of personality-based leadership. A more cognitive approach, by contrast, focuses on the message, the purposes, the values—the ideas that operate, in a way, as substitutes for leadership. Using ideas to back up leadership is an effective strategy because of its enduring nature.

8

Styles, Dispositions, and
Stages Count Too

Musings: How can we get Bob to exercise more leadership in his school and to exercise it in a way that helps us achieve our vision? I know his situation is tough, but he seems so obsessed with rules and regulations and so bogged down in the day-by-day running of his school that he often misses the point. Martha, on the other hand, is just the opposite. She is all vision but can't seem to get that vision into the real world. Doesn't she understand that visions count only after they generate actions that lead to their implementation? I wish that Betty was a little more independent. She is terrific at bringing people together, at finding the ways and means to get things done, and at empowering teachers so that they want to lead and lead well. But I am not sure she gets it. I have to stay on top of things at her school, reminding her of what our master plan is. She puts together the right teams but still there is no overall direction. There is no big picture to bring everything together. She needs to make instructional coherence a priority in her school. And to do this she not only needs to develop a sense of direction but a framework of assumptions, principles, and beliefs that is greater than the sum of its parts.

Some might say that maybe we need to redouble our efforts in providing Bob, Martha, Betty, and other members of the administrative team with more and better leadership training. That seems logical enough. Leadership is important. But not everyone agrees it is that important. Some believe, for example, that leaders bring immutable styles and dispositions to their practice—styles and dispositions that have their roots in personality. Instead of saying "The administrative team needs better training," their advice would be "We need to get better at selecting the right people for the right job." Different approaches to leadership work for different purposes and in different contexts. As purposes and contexts change, so should leadership.

Patricia Pitcher (1997), who is professor of leadership at Montreal's École des Hautes Études Commerciales, represents the second view. She would not deny that leadership training counts but makes the point that personality factors, dispositions, and styles or *archetypes* of leadership count too—and count a lot.

The Three Archetypes

Over a period of eight years Pitcher studied fifteen key executives in a global financial corporation. She was interested in the links between leadership, personality type, and organizational effectiveness. Yes, there is a hazard in transferring findings about leadership from the corporate world to the world of schooling. And when the research base for these findings is a case study of a single organization, we have to be even more careful. With these caveats in mind, Pitcher's revelations about leadership are helpful—because the archetypes she proposes are familiar to us (see, for example, Blumberg, 1988). The other reason is that her findings make intuitive sense when applied to our situation.

Pitcher's study revealed three archetypes: *artists* who were brilliant visionaries, people oriented, open minded, and intuitive; *craftsmen* who were empathetic and effective developers of people, who empowered others, and who were skilled at bringing out the best in others; and *technocrats* who though often brilliant were prone to place hyper-rationality over emotions and though meticulous and superb at managing things had difficulty managing people effectively. Technocrats were prone to use an approach to management that resembles painting by the numbers. Each of the three types brings strengths to any organization if properly matched to the right roles and responsibilities. Mismatched placements, Pitcher found in her study, were a recipe for disaster.

As most of us search our experience it is likely that we are able to recall mismatched placements. Lucy, for example, was a successful principal in the suburban fringe of the district. Her school was always rated on top and teachers did what they could to snag transfers to that school. But when Lucy was moved to another school closer to the center of town she failed miserably.

Since Pitcher uses familiar language to describe the archetypes, it is easier to apply them. For example, most of us know that though artist visionary leaders are important, they alone are rarely able to hold things together. They may build a lovely house of cards, but it is likely to tumble down soon after they leave. Artists who surround themselves with craftsmen, however, are able to change their associates' connections from them and their charisma to ideas, frameworks, and implementation routines.

Craftsman Leaders Are Critical

Craftsmen are key because they know how to turn visions into reality, to take big ideas and make them understandable and useful, and to bring together the right mix of human resources to make schools work. Dan, Eric, and John, the administrators from Stevenson High School discussed in Chapter Six, are examples of expert craftsmen leaders. To assume the craftsman role effectively, leaders need to master the eight basic competencies proposed and discussed in Chapter Seven. Craftsmen are good at managing attention, managing meaning, managing trust, managing self, managing paradox, and managing effectiveness. Let artists sketch out the visions and craftsmen will change them into realities.

Even technocrats are part of our history in schools. Sitting on a mountain of rules and regulations, leaders from this archetype seek to lead by using a kind of management that is both scripted and impersonal. That technocrats are powerful is evidenced by the unprecedented standardization of teaching and learning, the ultra-rational alignment of teaching and learning with standards and tests, and the overuse of cookie-cutter curriculum and teaching packages that now seem to characterize our everyday world of schooling. Sure, standards and tests are important, but technocrats are typically blind to any other learnings.

In many schools we have too much vision and not enough people who can build strategies, develop programs, and marshal human resources to get the job done. We need more craftsmen. We could also probably do with fewer technocrats even though they have important, albeit limited, roles to play. Pitcher worries about the proliferation of technocrats in top leadership roles, arguing that while such leaders are useful lower in the organization or off to the side, they can do irreparable harm should they reach the principal's office or the superintendent's office.

Artists view leadership as *vision,* which transfers ideas into goals. Craftsmen view leadership as *design,* which transfers ideas into things. And technocrats view leadership as a *script* that transfers ideas into rules, steps, and procedures. Artists, says Pitcher, are inclined to be emotional, imaginative, and entrepreneur-like. Craftsmen are inclined to be stable, wise, and responsible. And technocrats are inclined to be serious, meticulous, and methodical.

Leadership as vision, design, and script are all needed to make things work in schools. Thus the issue is not whether any of the three should be included or not but how and where they should be distributed in a school or a school district.

What Kind of Leader Are You?

Think about the cadre of designated leaders in your schools and the cadre of designated leaders in your school district. What percentage of them could be labeled as artists? What percentage could be labeled as craftsmen? And what percentage as technocrats? Which of the archetypes best describes you? Try rating yourself on the

"What Kind of Leader Are You?" inventory that appears in Table 8.1. Distribute ten points across each group of three adjectives, awarding points to reflect the way the adjectives fit you. If all three adjectives seem to apply fairly equally, give two of them three points and the third 4 points. If one fits the bill exactly and the other two are clearly off the track, give the one ten points and the others none. Once your points are distributed, find the sum for each of the three archetypes. If the total for any of the archetypes is fifty or more, there is a strong likelihood that this archetype fits you well. Don't be surprised if two archetypes seem to be weighted substantially more than the third. Keep in mind that reflection and conversation are the purpose of this inventory, not measurement per se.

What does it mean if your technocrat score is high relative to the other two? Only that you are inclined to want to organize things and get them scripted in a way that makes them easier for you to control, and this makes you more comfortable. High artist scores and high craftsman scores work similarly. As pointed out earlier, artists are good at the vision thing and feel most comfortable when they are so involved. And craftsmen are good at figuring out how visions will become realities. The difference is in how these types are distributed in your school. If there are too many artists, too many technocrats, or not enough craftsmen, you can expect problems. Craftsmen are key to making things work. Without them nothing happens.

As you think back over this book's first seven chapters, you will note the importance of leadership as design and note that the work of craftsmen is critical to a school's success. They are at the heart of leading and learning together. Chapter Two's proposal that leadership should be regarded as an entitlement is an example. People earn the right to lead, regardless of their position, if they have the necessary competence and skill and make the necessary commitment that helps get things done. In Chapter Three it was noted that to make visions useful they need to be transferred into action statements that outline the responsibilities each constituent group in a school has in helping to achieve the school's vision. In Chapter Five

Table 8.1. What Kind of Leader Are You?

Artist		Craftsman		Technocrat		Points Available
Unpredictable	____	Well-balanced	____	Cerebral	____	= 10
Funny	____	Helpful	____	Difficult	____	= 10
Imaginative	____	Honest	____	Uncompromising	____	= 10
Daring	____	Sensible	____	Stiff	____	= 10
Intuitive	____	Responsible	____	Intense	____	= 10
Exciting	____	Trustworthy	____	Detail-oriented	____	= 10
Emotional	____	Realistic	____	Determined	____	= 10
Visionary	____	Steady	____	Fastidious	____	= 10
Entrepreneurial	____	Reasonable	____	Hardheaded	____	= 10
Inspiring	____	Predictable	____	No-nonsense	____	= 10
Sum for Artist = ____		Sum for Craftsman = ____		Sum for Technocrat = ____		TOTALS = 100

Note: Take ten points and distribute them across each group of three adjectives, assigning points to reflect the way the adjectives fit you. Follow the other instructions provided in the text. Please note that the purpose of this inventory is to help readers engage in reflection and conversation about the leadership archetypes as they apply to you and to others. No presumption is made that the archetypes and the personality categories underlying them will be accurately measured.

Source: The archetypes and their descriptions, but not the inventory directions and format itself, are from Pitcher, 1997, p. 4. Used by permission of John Wiley & Sons, Inc. For a more accurate measurement of the archetypes, see the Pitcher Adjective Types (PAT) Inventory and the accompanying discussion that appears on pp. 205–210 of Pitcher's book.

it was noted that a student-centered focus needs to be embedded in a framework of teacher-centeredness that honors teachers' skills, provides them with support, encourages their learning, and provides them with the discretion they need to practice well. In Chapter Six it was noted that communities of practice bubble up and collaborative cultures trickle down to strengthen the competence and will of teachers, and to encourage them to work together more effectively in teaching and learning. In Chapter Seven the theme was that leadership works best when it uses ideas (purposes and commitments, promises, valid theories, and frameworks) as a source of authority, and using ideas effectively requires the mastery of eight basic competencies—competencies that define the work of craftsmen.

Sure, artists have a role to play by providing the initial spark, but it is craftsmen that create the designs, marshal the human resources, and in other ways move the school along. They even help technocrats get their acts together by linking their management skills with the designs for action needed to make the school work. If you have too many artists and too many technocrats, they wind up impeding progress by getting the school bogged down in theory as an end in itself or with management scripts that box people in, make decisions for them, and in other ways reduce their ability to work effectively.

There is no formula that will tell you what the right distribution of leadership should be among the three archetypes. But my guess is something like 10 percent artists, 10 percent technocrats, and 80 percent craftsmen might work in most cases. Pitcher summarizes the situation in these terms: "We believe that human progress has a poetic phase, which corresponds to art, and a scientific phase, which here corresponds to technique, it also has a craft phase, where what is found with art comes into use and is transformed, perfected, refined, concretized, shaped, sculpted by experience" (1997, p. 227). Taking this message to heart suggests that the real heroes in schools are not the visionaries at all but the people who are able to make those visions a reality. Sometimes they are the same person but often they are different persons. Craftsmen may not be flashy. They may not get as much attention as they should, and they may not be as exciting to be with—but you can count on them to make things work well for students every day.

Leadership and Student Achievement

What does leadership that correlates with student achievement look like? Are the responsibilities, understandings, and behaviors of leaders who are effective at promoting student achievement more likely to be found among artists, craftsmen, or technocrats? In a recent McREL meta-analysis of more than five thousand studies completed since 1970, researchers Tim Waters, Robert Marzano, and Brian McNulty identified twenty-one "leadership responsibilities" that were significantly correlated with student achievement. The ten leadership responsibilities with the strongest correlations are described in the following list (summarized from Waters, Marzano, and McNulty, 2003, p. 4 and pp. 9–12). Average correlation for each responsibility is provided in parenthesis. Student effectiveness is correlated with the extent to which the leader

- Understands the dynamic of how schools work by being aware of relationships among staff as well as the issues that could cause discord and uses this information to address existing problems and to prevent new problems (.33)

- Makes staff aware of current theories and research frameworks by routinely engaging staff in discussions and providing opportunities to learn and use best practices (.32)

- Actively challenges the status quo by leading change even when outcomes are uncertain and by considering new ways to do things (.30)

- Rallies staff around beliefs, fostering cooperation and building community that results in a shared understanding of purpose and a shared vision of what the school can be (.29)

- Is an advocate and spokesperson for the school with central office, parents, and other stakeholders (.28)

- Monitors and evaluates the effects of such school practices as curriculum development and delivery, teaching and learning, and assessment (.28)

- Provides for class structures, rules, and procedures for students and staff and establishes routines for running the school (.26)

- Ensures that teachers have the staff development, materials, and equipment they need to be effective in the classroom (.26)

- Systematically recognizes and celebrates accomplishments of teachers and students and acknowledges failures (.25)

- Routinely communicates and operates from strong ideals and beliefs about schools and about teaching and learning (.25)

These responsibilities and practices of effective leaders include attention to vision but it is the details of follow-up and the importance of building collaborative cultures within the school that carry the day. As you examine these responsibilities and practices, which of the archetypes seems to be at the center and which seems to be at the periphery? I am betting your choices will lead you to the conclusion that craftsman leaders who have the knowledge, skills, commitment, and disposition to transfer vision into realities are critical to success.

Here is how the McREL researchers sum things up:

> Effective leadership means more than simply knowing
> what to do—it's knowing when, how, and why to do it.
> Effective leaders understand how to balance pushing for
> change while at the same time protecting aspects of cul-
> ture, values, and norms worth preserving. They know
> which policies, practices, resources, and incentives to
> align and how to align them with organizational priori-
> ties. They know how to gauge the magnitude of change
> they are calling for and how to tailor their leadership
> strategies accordingly. Finally, they understand and value
> the people in the organization. They know when, how,
> and why to create learning environments that support
> people, connect them with one another, and provide the
> knowledge, skills, and resources they need to succeed.
> This combination of knowledge and skills is the essence
> of balanced leadership [Waters, Marzano, and McNulty,
> 2003, p. 2].

The Stages of Leadership

As I've said before, different approaches to leadership work for different purposes and in different contexts, and as those purposes and
contexts change, so should leadership. Recent research by the Center on Reinventing Public Education (2003), for example, indicates
that "a 'one-size-fits-all' posture toward leadership training or methods and styles of school leadership serves neither principals nor
schools well" (p. 1). This report argues that "districts that treat leaders as interchangeable are likely to pay a price in ineffective schooling. Instead . . . districts need to assign principals to schools that can
make best use of their particular leadership skills and style" (p. 1).

The leadership route to school improvement is in many ways
developmental. This route comprises four stages with value-added

leadership playing an important role.[1] You might get by with stages 1 and 2, but if your goal is excellence you will need to reach stages 3 and 4 as well. The leader can begin the process at any of the stages depending upon the preceding stages that are or are not in place. Principals of "turnaround" schools, for example, typically began their quest for excellence at the first stage. By contrast, principals of schools that are functioning competently but not to full potential often begin their quest at stages 2 or 3. Since not every leader is equally effective in all of the stages, the issue in many cases becomes one of fit. Some "turnaround principals," for example, have neither the style nor disposition to be successful at other stages. And moving to other stages may require a change in leadership. The stages are as follows:

Stage 1, *Bartering:* Leader and led strike a bargain within which leader gives to led something they want in exchange for something the leader wants.

Stage 2, *Building:* Leader provides the climate and interpersonal support that enhances opportunities for fulfillment of needs for achievement, responsibility, competence, and esteem.

Stage 3, *Binding:* Leader and led develop a set of shared values and commitments that provides direction and gives meaning and significance to what is done.

Stage 4, *Bonding:* Leader and led are bonded together in community that changes their relationships and changes their commitment in such a way that school improvements are institutionalized into the everyday life of the school.

---

[1] This chapter discusses the four stages of leadership as they appeared in Chapter Three of *Value-Added Leadership.* In the original the four stages were bartering, building, bonding, and banking. Banking has been replaced by binding, and the order has been adjusted. I now understand that the bonding of people is usually the result of their being bound to shared values and ideas. Thus, the four stages are now bartering, building, binding, and bonding.

James MacGregor Burns (1978) introduced a set of ideas that has influenced how leadership is now understood. According to Burns, leadership is exercised when persons with certain motives and purposes mobilize resources so as to arouse and satisfy the motives of followers. He identified two kinds of leadership, transactional and transformative. *Transactional* leadership focuses on basic and largely extrinsic motives and needs, while *transformative* leadership focuses on higher-order, more intrinsic motives and needs.

In transactional leadership, leaders and followers exchange needs and services in order to accomplish independent objectives. The objectives may be related but they are separate nonetheless. This exchange process can be viewed metaphorically as a form of *leadership by bartering*. The wants and needs of followers and the wants and needs of the leader are traded and a bargain is struck. Positive reinforcement is given for good work, merit pay for increased performance, promotion for increased persistence, a feeling of belonging for cooperation, and so on.

In transformative leadership, by contrast, leaders and followers are united in pursuit of higher-level goals that are common to both. Both want to become the best. Both want to shape the school in a new direction. In Burns's words, "Such leadership occurs when one or more persons engage with others in such a way that leaders and followers raise one another to higher levels of motivation and morality" (1978, p. 20). When transformative leadership is practiced, purposes that might have started out as separate, as in the case of transactional leadership, come together. Initially transformative leadership takes the form of *leadership by building*. Here the focus is on arousing human potential, satisfying higher needs, and raising expectations of both leader and follower in a manner that motivates both to higher levels of commitment and performance.

Leadership by bartering responds to basic physical, security, social, and ego needs. Leadership by building responds to more powerful needs such as esteem, achievement, competence, autonomy, and self-actualization. The leadership concepts associated with leadership by bartering are the development of management skills, using appropriate leadership styles, and applying the principles of situational leadership theory. The principles associated with leadership by building are empowerment, symbolic leadership, and charisma.

Burns points out that ultimately transformative leadership becomes moral because it raises the level of human conduct and ethical aspiration of both leader and led; thus it has a transforming effect on both. When this occurs transformative leadership takes the forms of *leadership by binding and bonding*. Here the focus is on arousing awareness and consciousness that elevate school goals and purposes to the level of a shared covenant to which leaders and others are bound in a moral commitment. Leadership by binding responds to such intrinsic human needs as the desire for purpose, meaning, and significance in what one does. The key concepts associated with leadership by binding are cultural and moral leadership.

Leadership by bartering, building, binding, and bonding, when viewed sequentially, form stages of leadership for school improvement. Bartering provides the push needed to get things started; building provides the support needed to deal with uncertainty; and binding provides the sources of authority and the inspiration needed for performance and commitment that is beyond expectations. A school improvement effort becomes real only when it becomes institutionalized as part of the everyday life of the school. And this goal is best achieved when principals and teachers come together in community. To this effort *leadership by bonding* becomes the fourth stage of school improvement. Bonding seeks to routinize school improvements by connecting people together in ways that make them a part of a school's culture of support, belonging, and long-term commitment that ensures bonds of trust.[2]

---

[2] In *Beyond Rational Management*, Robert E. Quinn (1988) proposes a similar four-stage cycle (initialization, uncertainty, transformation, and routinization) to describe how a person or group achieves excellence or peak experience.

The Stages in Action

Each of the stages of leadership serves as an overall school-improvement *strategy*. However, *tactically* speaking, bartering, building, binding, and bonding are leadership *styles* that can be used simultaneously for different purposes or different people. A recalcitrant principal, teacher, or student, for example, will likely require leadership by bartering regardless of the overall strategy you follow.

The four stages of leadership for school improvement were illustrated in *Value-Added Leadership* by the leadership practices of Jane Kendrick, who was at the time principal of the Henry J. Eggers Middle School in Hammond, Indiana. The four stages are alive and well at Stevenson High School and at hundreds of successful schools across the country. Talking about stages of leadership as if they were rigid and fixed categories simplifies things too much. Suffice to say that school improvement has a beginning and an end. When successful, the beginning is usually at the bartering stage and the end is usually at the bonding stage. Usually not everyone is at the same place at the same time. Thus different stages are emphasized for different people, for different issues, and for different times.

Leading and Learning Together

Leaders both represent the values of the group and determine the values of the group (Greenfield, 1984). There is a social order within which schools function. Leaders and schools, for example, take their cue from state governments, local school boards, professional associations, and other entities that function as sources of authority. Schools are obliged, as well, to pay heed to those in positions higher than theirs. This social order compels designated leaders to lead by defining purposes and setting the course of action. As Barnard (1938) saw it, leaders are the embodiment of the organization's central purpose, and this role obligates them to seek the commitment of others to these purposes. Greenfield (1984) puts it this way: "The leader cannot escape deciding, even if the decision is only to decide not to decide" (p. 164).

There is no easy reconciliation of the conflict between leaders as representative of group values and leaders as deciders of group goals. The only way out is to blend the two. Superintendents, for example, blend the two when their relationship to others is that of first among equals. Principals too can be first among equals in their relationships with teachers. Being first among equals means actively taking the lead while actively enabling others to lead. Enabling others involves building their capacity and commitment and in other ways putting them in a position where they become entitled to lead. An important part of the principal's job and the superintendent's job is to provide the conditions for this to happen and to guide the process and outcomes of decision making so that they are consistent with the school's purposes. As Peter Drucker (2000) sees it, "The means . . . [to achieving our purposes and getting the results we want] is knowledge, which is owned by knowledge workers . . . Knowledge workers provide 'capital' just as much as does the provider of money. The two are dependent on each other" (pp. 273–274).

If our craftsman leaders were to explain their practice in Drucker's terms, it is likely that they would point to two kinds of capital that they seek to build: knowledge capital, which is what we know and what we can do, and social capital, which is the support and relational trust we willingly get and freely give. Both kinds of capital are needed to create collaborative cultures that are purpose driven and both are needed to help grow communities of practice that take collegiality to the next level. Drucker continues, "This makes the knowledge worker an equal—an associate of the partner" (p. 274). There is no other way to lead and learn together.

Why together? Because the greatest asset a school has is its collective intelligence. Leaders have to figure out how to harness this intelligence, to grow it, and to use it to help achieve the school's purposes. Too often this intelligence is divided among individuals, diluting its effectiveness. Thus school leadership should not just be about making individuals smarter for their own sake. It should also be about making schools smarter. Schools get smarter when individual intelligences are aggregated.

References

Anderson, S., and Togneri, W. "Building Instructional Leadership: A Case Study of the Providence Public School Department." Washington, D.C.: Learning First Alliance, May 2003.

Association for Supervision and Curriculum Development. "An 'Insider's' View of ASCD: What's Behind ASCD's What Works in Schools Program." *Associate News*, Winter 2003.

Barnard, C. I. *The Functions of the Executive*. Cambridge, Mass.: Harvard University Press, 1938.

Barth, R. "The Principal and the Profession of Teaching." In T. J. Sergiovanni and J. H. Moore (eds.), *Schooling for Tomorrow: Directing Reforms to Issues That Count*. Boston: Allyn & Bacon, 1989.

Bennis, W. "Transformative Power and Leadership." In T. J. Sergiovanni and J. E. Corbally (eds.), *Leadership and Organizational Culture*. Urbana: University of Illinois Press, 1984.

Bennis, W. *Why Leaders Can't Lead: The Unconscious Conspiracy Continues*. San Francisco: Jossey-Bass, 1989.

Bennis, W., and Nanus, B. *Leaders: The Strategies for Taking Charge*. New York: HarperCollins, 1985.

Blumberg, A. *School Administration as Craft: Foundations of Practice*. Boston: Allyn & Bacon, 1988.

Bolman, L., and Deal, T. *Leading with Soul: An Uncommon Journey of Spirit*. San Francisco: Jossey-Bass, 1995.

Brackenridge Forum for the Enhancement of Teaching. *Teachers Speak: Quality Schooling for Texas Today and Tomorrow*. San Antonio, Tex.: Trinity University, 1987.

Bronowski, J. *The Origins of Knowledge and Imagination*. New Haven, Conn.: Yale University Press, 1978.

Bryk, A. S., and Driscoll, M. E. *The School as Community: Theoretical Foundations, Contextual Influences and Consequences for Teachers and Students*. Madison, Wis.: National Center for Effective Secondary Schools, 1988.

Bryk, A. S., and Schneider, B. *Trust in Schools: A Core Resource for Improvement*. New York: Russell Sage Foundation, 2002.

Bryk, A. S., and Schneider, B. "Trust in Schools: A Core Resource for School Reform." *Educational Leadership*, 2003, 60(6), 40–44.

Bunting, C. "Quiet Transformations: Good Teachers Are the Key to Everything." *Education Week*, April 9, 2003, p. 41.

Burns, J. M. *Leadership*. New York: HarperCollins, 1978.

Carey, G. N., and Frohnen, B. (eds.) *Community and Tradition: Conservative Perspectives on the American Experience*. Lanham, Md.: Rowman & Littlefield, 1998.

Carlyle, T. *Sartor Resartus: The Life and Opinions of Herr Tefelsdröckh*. (C. F. Harrold, ed.). New York: Odyssey Press, 1937.

Carnegie Forum on Education and the Economy. *A Nation Prepared: Teachers for the 21st Century*. New York: Carnegie Corporation, 1986.

Carter, L. "A Role for Hope in Today's Leadership Challenge?" *Hopewatch: Newsletter of the Center for a Science of Hope*, 1996, (5), 1–4.

Center on Reinventing Public Education. "A Practical Look at School Leadership." Policy Brief, Sept. 10, 2003.

Chu, L. "MLK's Kin Say Not to Wait for a New Leader." *San Antonio Express-News,* Jan. 20, 2003, p. 3A.

Cohen, R. M. "Schools Our Teachers Deserve: A Proposal for Teacher-Centered Reform." *Phi Delta Kappan,* March 2002, pp. 532–537.

Cohen, R. M., and Sheer, S. *Teacher-Centered Schools: Reimagining Educational Reform in the 21st Century.* Lanham, Md.: Scarecrow Press, 2003.

Coleman, J. S. "Social Capital in the Creation of Human Capital." *American Journal of Sociology,* 1988, 94 (Supplement), S95-S120.

Comer, J. P. *School Power: Implications of an Intervention Program.* New York: Free Press, 1980.

Darling-Hammond, L. "Teacher Quality and Student Achievement: A Review of State Policy Evidence." *Educational Policy Analysis Archives,* 2000, 8(1), 1–50.

Deal, T. E., and Kennedy, A. A. *Corporate Cultures.* Reading, Mass.: Addison-Wesley, 1982.

Donaldson, G. A., Jr. *Cultivating Leadership in Schools: Connecting People, Purpose and Practice.* New York: Teachers College Press, 2001.

Drucker, P. *Managing in the Next Society.* New York: St. Martin's Press, 2000.

Druskat, V. U., and Wolff, S. B. "Building the Emotional Intelligence of Groups." *Harvard Business Review,* 2001, 79(3), 80–90.

Elmore, R. F. *Bridging the Gap Between Standards and Achievement: The Imperative for Professional Development in Education.* Washington, D.C.: Albert Shanker Institute, 2002.

Elmore, R. F. "A Plea for Strong Practice." *Educational Leadership,* 2003, 61(3), 6–10.

Epstein, J. L. *School, Family, and Community Partnerships: Preparing Educators and Improving Schools.* Boulder, Colo.: Westview Press, 2001.

Etzioni, A. "The Community of Communities." *The Responsive Community,* 1996/1997, *7*(1), 21–32.

Evans, R. *The Human Side of School Change: Reform, Resistance, and the Real-Life Problems of Innovation.* San Francisco: Jossey-Bass, 1996.

Ferguson, R. "Paying for Public Education: New Evidence on How and Why Money Matters." *Harvard Journal on Legislation,* 1991, *28*(2), 465–498.

Fuhrman, S. H. "Is 'Reform' the Answer for Urban Education?" *@ Penn GSE: A Review of Research.* Philadelphia: University of Pennsylvania, 2003.

Fullan, M., with S. Stiegelbauer. *The New Meaning of Educational Change.* (2nd ed.) New York: Teachers College Press, 1991.

Gardner, H. *Leading Minds: An Anatomy of Leadership.* New York: Basic Books, 1995.

Green, J. (ed.). *What Next? More Leverage for Teachers.* Denver, Colo.: Education Commission of the States, 1986.

Greenfield, T. B. "Leaders and Schools: Willfulness and Nonnatural Order in Organizations." In T. J. Sergiovanni and J. E. Corbally (eds.), *Leadership and Organizational Culture.* Urbana: University of Illinois Press, 1984.

Gregory, T. "Small Is Too Big: Achieving a Critical Anti-Mass in the High School." Position paper prepared for the Hubert H. Humphrey Institute for Public Affairs and the North Central Regional Educational Laboratory, Minneapolis, Minn., Sept. 1992.

Habermas, J. *The Theory of Communicative Action.* Vol. 2: *Lifeworld and System: A Critique of Functional Reason.* (T. McCarthy, trans.) Boston: Beacon Press, 1987.

Hage, J., and Powers, C. H. *Post-Industrial Lives: Roles and Relationships in the 21st Century.* Thousand Oaks, Calif.: Sage, 1992.

Hallinger, P., and Heck, R. "Reassessing the Principal's Role in School Effectiveness: A Review of Empirical Research 1980–1995." *Educational Administration Quarterly,* 1996a, *32*(1), 5–44.

Hallinger, P., and Heck, R. "The Principal's Role in School Effectiveness: A Review of Methodological Issues, 1980–1995." In K. Leithwood and others (eds.), *The International Handbook of Research in Educational Administration*. New York: Kluwer, 1996b.

Hallinger, P., and Heck, R. "Can Leadership Enhance School Effectiveness?" In T. Bush, L. Bell, R. Bolan, R. Glatter, and P. Ribbens (eds.), *Educational Management: Redefining Theory, Policy and Practice*. London: Paul Chapman, 1999.

Halpin, A. *Theory and Research in Administration*. New York: Macmillan, 1966.

Hargreaves, A. *Changing Teachers, Changing Times*. New York: Teachers College Press, 1994.

Hauser, S. "Leadership." *Rochester Review*, 2002, 59(1), 9.

Hayes, R. H. "Strategic Planning—Forward in Reverse?" *Harvard Business Review*, 1985, 63(6), 111–119.

Hill, P. T., and Celio, M. B. *Fixing Urban Schools*. Washington, D.C.: Brookings Institution Press, 1998.

Hill, P. T., Foster, G. E., and Gendler, T. *High Schools with Character*. Santa Monica, Calif.: RAND Corporation, 1990.

Hollenbach, D. "Virtue, the Common Good and Democracy." In A. Etzioni (ed.), *New Communitarian Thinking: Persons, Virtues, Institutions, and Communities*. Charlottesville: University Press of Virginia, 1995.

Hoyle, J. *Leadership and the Force of Love*. Thousand Oaks, Calif.: Corwin Press, 2002.

Huberman, M. "The Model of the Independent Artisan in Teachers' Professional Relations." In J. W. Little and M. W. McLaughlin (eds.), *Teachers' Work: Individuals, Colleagues, Contexts*. New York: Teachers College Press, 1993.

Hurst, D. K. "Of Boxes, Bubbles, and Effective Management." *Harvard Business Review*, 1984, 62(3), 78–88.

"Is Your Company Up to Speed?" *Fast Company*, June 2003, pp. 81–86.

Kant, I. *Foundations of the Metaphysics of Morals*. (L. W. Beck, trans.). Indianapolis, Ind.: Bobbs-Merril, 1959. (Originally published 1785.)

Kanter, R. M. *Men and Women of the Corporation*. New York: Basic Books, 1997.

Kearns, D. T. "A Business Perspective in American Schooling." *Education Week*, April 20, 1988, p. 24.

Kendall, D. M. "The Four Simple Truths of Management." *Vital Speeches*, May 15, 1986, 52(15), 475–478.

Kouzes, J. M., and Posner, B. Z. *The Leadership Challenge*. (3rd ed.) San Francisco: Jossey-Bass, 2003.

Lakoff, G., and Johnson, M. *Metaphors We Live By*. Chicago: University of Chicago Press, 1980.

Lambert, L. "Toward a Deepened Theory of Constructivist Leadership." In L. Lambert, and others, *The Constructivist Leader*. (2nd ed.) New York: Teachers College Press, 2002.

Lambert, L., and others. *The Constructivist Leader*. (2nd ed.), New York: Teachers College Press, 2002.

Langer, S. K. *Philosophy in a New Key: A Study of Symbolism of Reason, Rite, and Art*. Cambridge: Harvard University Press, 1978.

Lieberman, A., and Miller, L. *Teachers—Transforming Their World and Their Work*. New York: Teachers College Press, 1999.

Lightfoot, S. *The Good High School*. New York: Basic Books, 1983.

Lipsitz, J. *Successful Schools for Young Adolescents*. New Brunswick, N.J.: Transaction Books, 1984.

Little, J. W. "School Success and Staff Development in Urban Desegregated Schools." Boulder, Colo.: Center for Action Research, 1981.

MacBeath, J. *Schools Must Speak for Themselves: The Case for School Self-Evaluation*. London: Routledge, 1999.

March, J. G. "How We Talk and How We Act: Administrative Theory and Administrative Life." In T. J. Sergiovanni and J. E. Corbally (eds.), *Leadership and Organizational Culture*. Urbana: University of Illinois Press, 1984.

March, J. G., and Olsen, J. P. *Ambiguity and Choice in Organizations*. Bergen, Norway: Universitetstorlaget, 1976.

Marzano, R. J. *A New Era of School Reform: Going Where the Research Takes Us*. Aurora, Colo.: Mid-Continent Research for Educational Learning, 2000.

Marzano, R. J. *What Works in Schools: Translating Research into Action*. Alexandria, Va.: Association for Supervision and Curriculum Development, 2003.

McDermott, D., Pedrotti, J. T., Edwards, L. M., and Houske, A. M. "An Exploration of Hope in Catholic School Students." *Catholic Education: A Journal of Inquiry and Practice*, 2002, 5(3), 274–285.

McDonnell, L. M., and Elmore, R. F. "Getting the Job Done: Alternative Policy Instruments." *Educational Evaluation and Policy Analysis*, 1987, 9(2), 133–152.

McLaughlin, M., and Yee, M. "School as a Place to Have a Career." In A. Lieberman (ed.), *Building a Professional Culture in Schools*. New York: Teachers College Press, 1988.

Menninger, K., Mayman, M., and Pruyser, P. *The Vital Balance: The Life Process in Mental Health and Illness*. New York: Penguin Books, 1963.

Mintzberg, H., Ahlstrand, B., and Lampel, J. *Strategy Safari: A Guided Tour Through the Wilds of Strategic Management*. New York: Free Press, 1998.

National Governors' Association. *Time for Results: The Governors' 1986 Report on Education*. Washington, D.C.: National Governors' Association, 1986.

Newmann, F. M., Bryk, A. S., and Nagaoka, J. K. *Authentic Intellectual Work and Standardized Tests: Conflict or Coexistence?* Chicago: Consortium on Chicago School Research, 2001.

Newmann, F. M., Smith, B., Allensworth, E., and Bryk, A. S. "Instructional Program Coherence: What It Is and Why It Should Guide School Improvement Policy." *Educational Evaluation and Policy Analysis*, 2001, 23(4), 297–321.

Noddings, N. *The Challenge to Care in Schools: An Alternative Approach to Education.* New York: Teachers College Press, 1992.

Nothwehr, D. *Mutuality: A Formal Norm for Christian Social Ethics.* San Francisco: Catholic Scholars Press, 1998.

Peters, T. J., and Waterman, R. H., Jr. *In Search of Excellence: Lessons from America's Best-Run Companies.* New York: HarperCollins, 1982.

Peterson, K. "The Necessary Principal: The Importance of Instructional Leadership." *Curriculum Update,* Winter 2002, p. 3.

Pitcher, P. *The Drama of Leadership: Artists, Craftsmen, and Technocrats and the Power Struggle That Shapes Organizations and Societies.* New York: Wiley, 1997.

Puriefoy, W. "Newsblast Special Edition: Give Kids Good Schools." *Public Education Network,* Jan. 7, 2003, n.p.

Putnam, R. D. *Bowling Alone.* New York: Simon & Schuster, 2000.

Quinn, J. B. "Formulating Strategy One Step at a Time." *Journal of Business Strategy,* 1981, *1*(3), 92–107.

Quinn, R. E. *Beyond Rational Management.* San Francisco: Jossey-Bass, 1988.

Rensis Likert Associates. "The Profile of a School." Ann Arbor, Mich.: Rensis Likert Associates, 1977.

Resnick, L. B., and Glennan, T. K., Jr. "Leadership for Learning: A Theory of Action for Urban School Districts." Pittsburgh: Institute for Learning, 2001. Available online: http://www.instituteforlearning.org/media/docs/ TheoryofActionResnickGlenna.pdf. Access date: Jan. 22, 2004.

Rinaldi, C. "Foreword." In L. B. Cadwell, *Bringing Learning to Life: The Reggio Approach to Early Childhood Education.* New York: Teachers College Press, 2003.

Roset, S. M. "Exploring Hope: Implications for Educational Leaders." Master of Education Thesis, Department of Educational Administration, University of Saskatchewan, 1999.

Rowan, B. "Commitment and Control: Alternative Strategies for the Organizational Design of Schools." *Review of Research in Education*, 1990, *16*, 353–389.

Samuel Gompers Elementary School. 2000–2001 Blue Ribbon Schools Program Application, Gompers School, Detroit, Michigan, 2000.

Sanders, W. L., and Horn, S. P. "The Tennessee Value-Added Assessment System (TVAAS) Mixed-Model Methodology in Educational Assessment." *Journal of Personnel Evaluation in Education*, 1994, *8*, 299–311.

Sebring, P. B., and Bryk, A. S. "Student-Centered Learning Climate." In P. B. Sebring and others, *Charting Reform in Chicago: The Students Speak*. Report sponsored by the Consortium of Chicago School Research. Chicago: University of Chicago, 1996.

Sebring, P. B., and others. *Charting Reform: Chicago Teachers Take Stock*. Report sponsored by the Consortium Chicago School Research. Chicago: University of Chicago, 1995.

Sebring, P. B., and others. *Charting Reform in Chicago: The Students Speak*. Report sponsored by the Consortium of Chicago School Research. Chicago: University of Chicago, 1996.

Selznick, P. "On a Communitarian Faith." *Responsive Community*, 2002, *12*(3), 67–74.

Senge, P. *The Fifth Discipline: The Art and Practice of the Learning Organization*. New York: Doubleday, 1990.

Sergiovanni, T. J. "Landscapes, Mindscapes, and Reflective Practice in Supervision." *Journal of Curriculum and Supervision*, 1985, *1*(1), 5–18.

Sergiovanni, T. J. *Value-Added Leadership: How to Get Extraordinary Performance in Schools*. San Diego: Harcourt Brace Jovanovich, 1990.

Sergiovanni, T. J. *Moral Leadership*. San Francisco: Jossey-Bass, 1992.

Sergiovanni, T. J. *Building Community in Schools*. San Francisco: Jossey-Bass, 1994.

Sergiovanni, T. J. *Leadership for the Schoolhouse*. San Francisco: Jossey-Bass, 1996.

Sergiovanni, T. J. *The Lifeworld of Leadership: Creating Culture, Community, and Personal Meaning in Our Schools*. San Francisco: Jossey-Bass, 2000.

Sergiovanni, T. J. *Leadership: What's in It for Schools?* London: Routledge Falmer, 2001.

Sergiovanni, T. J. "Idea-Based Leadership as a Focus for School Improvement." *Journal for Effective Schools*, 2003, 2(1), 17–21.

Sergiovanni, T. J., and Starratt, R. J. *Supervision: A Redefinition*. (7th ed.) New York: McGraw-Hill, 2002.

Shaffer, D. J. "Perot Talks Tough About Hard Times." *San Antonio Light*, March 1, 1988, pp. B1, B8.

Shils, E. A. "Centre and Periphery." In *The Logic of Personal Knowledge: Essays Presented to Michael Polanyi*. London: Routledge & Kegan Paul, 1961.

Shulman, L. S. "Teaching Alone, Learning Together: Needed Agendas for the New Reforms." In T. J. Sergiovanni and J. H. Moore (eds.), *Schooling for Tomorrow: Directing Reforms to Issues That Count*. Boston: Allyn & Bacon, 1989.

Smedes, L. *Standing on the Promises: Keeping Hope Alive for a Tomorrow We Cannot Control*. Nashville, Tenn.: Nelson, 1998.

Snyder, C. R., and others. "The Will and the Ways: Development and Validation of an Individual-Differences Measure of Hope." *Journal of Personality and Social Psychology*, 1991, 60(4), 570–585.

Spillane, J. P., Halverson, R., and Diamond, J. B. "Investigating School Leadership Practice: A Distributive Perspective." *Educational Researcher*, 2001, 30(3), 24.

Spindler, L. S. *Culture Change and Modernization: Mini-Models and Case Studies*. Prospect Heights, Ill.: Waveland Press, 1984.

Starratt, R. J. *Transforming Educational Administration: Meaning, Community, and Excellence*. New York: McGraw-Hill, 1996.

Sternberg, R. J. "What Is Successful Intelligence?" *Education Week,* Nov. 13, 1996, p. 48.

Stevenson High School. Vision statement and collective commitments by Stevenson's students, parents, faculty, staff, and school board, Jan. 2003. Available online: http://district125.K12.il.us/docs/vision.html. Access date: Jan. 28, 2004.

Stewart, T. A. *Intellectual Capital: The New Wealth of Organizations.* New York: Doubleday, 1997.

Susan B. Anthony Center for Women's Leadership. "Susan B. Anthony and Elizabeth Cady Stanton." Rochester, N.Y.: Susan B. Anthony Center for Women's Leadership, 2002a. Available online: http://www.rochester.edu/SBA/sbaecs.html. Access date: Jan. 22, 2004.

Susan B. Anthony Center for Women's Leadership. "151 Years Later: The Power of Their Friendship: Susan B. Anthony and Elizabeth Cady Stanton." Rochester, N.Y.: Susan B. Anthony Center for Women's Leadership, 2002b. Available online: http://www.rochester.edu/SBA/friendship/friendship.html. Access date: Jan. 22, 2004.

Szabo, M., and Lambert, L. "The Preparation of New Constructivist Leaders." In L. Lambert and others, *The Constructivist Leader.* (2nd ed.) New York: Teachers College Press, 2002.

Tannenbaum, A. *Control in Organizations.* New York: McGraw-Hill, 1968.

Thompson, V. A. *Modern Organization.* New York: Knopf, 1965.

"To Close the Gap, Quality Counts." *Education Week,* Jan. 9, 2003, p. 10.

Vaill, P. "The Purposing of High-Performing Systems." In T. J. Sergiovanni and J. E. Corbally (eds.), *Leadership and Organizational Culture.* Urbana: University of Illinois Press, 1984.

Valenzuela, A. *Subtractive Schooling: U.S.-Mexican Youth and the Politics of Caring.* Albany: State University of New York Press, 1999.

Viadero, D. "Analysis Teases Out Ways Principals Boost Learning." *Education Week,* Oct. 1, 2003, p. 7.

Walton, C. C. *The Moral Manager*. Cambridge, Mass.: Ballinger, 1988.

Waters, T., Marzano, R., and McNulty, B. "Balanced Leadership: What 30 Years of Research Tells Us About the Effects of Leadership on Student Achievement." Working paper, McREL, 2003. For information contact Resource Center at info@mcrel.org.

Weick, K. E. "Educational Organization as Loosely Coupled Systems." *Administrative Science Quarterly*, 1976, *21*(1), 1–19.

Weick, K. E. "Administering Education in Loosely Coupled Schools." *Phi Delta Kappan*, 1982, 63(10), 673–676.

"What Does the Swing of a Golf Club or Baseball Bat Have in Common with Good Management?" *American Way*, July 15, 2003, pp. 70–76.

Wilkins, A. L. *Developing Corporate Character: How to Successfully Change an Organization Without Destroying It*. San Francisco: Jossey-Bass, 1989.

Wise, A. E. *Legislated Learning: The Bureaucratization of the American Classroom*. Berkeley: University of California Press, 1979.

Wright, S. P., Horn, S., and Sanders, W. "Teacher and Classroom Context Effects on Student Achievement: Implications for Teacher Evaluation." *Journal of Personnel Evaluation in Education*, 1997, *11*(1), 57–67.

Index

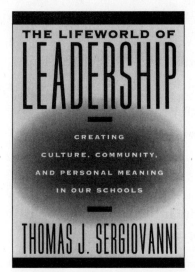

Other Books of Interest by Thomas J. Sergiovanni

The Lifeworld of Leadership: Creating Culture, Community, and Personal Meaning in Our Schools

"Sergiovanni gets to the heart of school reform and renewal in this book. He shows how local school communities can construct standards that support serious learning and effective caring for students. This is a must read for anyone involved in education policy or practice today."

—Linda Darling-Hammond, professor of education, Stanford University, codirector, National Center for Restructuring Education, Schools, and Teaching, Teachers College, Columbia University

At a time when sweeping educational mandates, systems requirements, and political conflicts seem to besiege our schools, it becomes clear that school leaders are most effective when they act according to the unique culture, values, and needs of their schools. In this inspiring book, Thomas J. Sergiovanni examines why the "lifeworld" of schools is so vital to school success and shows how local leadership can make the difference in creating healthy, rigorous schools for our children. *The Lifeworld of Leadership* explores the crucial link between school character and school improvement. By building institutional character at the local level, principals, superintendents, and policymakers can not only protect the lifeworld of their schools but also craft an educational system based on layered loyalties and shared accountability. Sergiovanni draws from an exhaustive review of school reform initiatives in the United States, Canada, the United Kingdom, Australia, and New Zealand to provide specific and compelling examples of local school leadership at its best. He proposes initiatives that invite all educational stakeholders to lead without compromising the legitimate interests of their schools and communities.

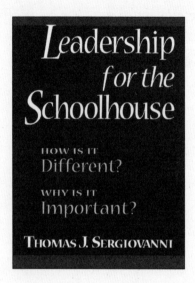

Leadership for the Schoolhouse: How Is It Different? Why Is It Important?

"Sergiovanni gives educators a powerful template for crafting responsible and humane schools."
—**Educational Leadership**

"The first book I've seen in years that provides an authentic organization for our schools—one reflecting their core purposes, functions, and rhythms. Reading this book will make educators feel they have come home to familiar land and can still build anew from there."
—**Michael Huberman,** professor, Graduate School of Education, Harvard University

Education guru Thomas Sergiovanni debunks the popular belief that leadership practices from the corporate world can be readily applied to schools. Schools are responsible for more than developing basic competence in students—they are also responsible for teaching habits of the mind and heart. Everything that happens in the schoolhouse has moral overtones that are virtually unmatched by other institutions in our society. This book provides educators with a leadership model that is based on what schools are like, what they are trying to do, and who they serve. This unique brand of leader-ship is more community-like, more democratic, and more responsive both to what we know about human nature and what we know about how students learn and develop. It replaces the politics of division—which emphasizes contracts and deals, and winning and losing—with the politics of virtue, which emphasizes a shared commitment to the common good. Drawing on ideas and stories from a variety of real schools, *Leadership for the Schoolhouse* provides a compelling picture of schooling and leadership at their best.

Building Community in Schools

"Provides the practitioner with both a theoretical blueprint with which to build learning communities and a rich supply of benchmark illustrations to use as prototypes. . . . Thought-provoking and challenging."
—**NASSP Bulletin**

"Sergiovanni is the leading writer in pushing us deeper and deeper toward understanding and creating a 'community of learners.'"
—**Michael Fullan,** dean of education, University of Toronto

"Sergiovanni does not just extol the virtues of educational communities. Through rich and vivid portraits, he conveys what they are like and how we might create them."

—**Howard Gardner,** professor of education and co-director of Project Zero, Harvard University

Both in and out of schools, people are experiencing a loss of community. In this book, Thomas J. Sergiovanni explains why a sense of community is so vital to the success of any school and shows teachers, parents, and administrators what they can do to rebuild it. Filled with case studies and other school examples, *Building Community in Schools* provides the necessary intellectual framework for understanding the need to create communities that are inclusive, meaningful, and democratic.

Moral Leadership: Getting to the Heart of School Improvement

"*Moral Leadership* provides a vision of what could (and probably should) be. . . . It is loaded with substance, and the reader may want to revisit some sections for further reflection."

—**Educational Leadership**

Moral Leadership shows how creating a new leadership practice—one with a moral dimension built around purpose, values, and beliefs—can transform a school from an organization into a community and inspire the kinds of commitment, devotion, and service that can make our schools great. Sergiovanni explains the importance of legitimizing emotion and getting in touch with basic values and connections with others. He reveals how true collegiality, based on shared work and common goals, leads to a natural interdependence among teachers and shows how a public declaration of values and purpose can help turn schools into virtuous communities where teachers are self-managers and professionalism is considered an ideal.